LOVE YOU MORE

JUANITA MARIE SIMPSON

Copyright © 2020 by Juanita Marie Simpson

All rights reserved.

Published by Red Penguin Books

No part of this book may be reproduced in any form or by any electronic or mechanical means, including information storage and retrieval systems, without written permission from the author, except for the use of brief quotations in a book review.

Dedicated to Raymond Anthony Simpson, Sr.

I thank GOD for giving me the strength to write this book through the pain!
I thank GOD for our four adult children, Carla Elaina (aka Carlzbear), Alanna Marie (aka (LaniBani, RayJ (aka Superman), and Jonathan Ray (aka Bookyboy)
Mrs. Verdel J. (who I met many years ago, and didn't realize our husbands were co-workers/friends before we even met...)
Mrs. Michelle A. (for taking me out to lunch and encouraging me to write!)
And especially, Vivi and ShellyB, (who were with us from the beginning to the end)

1

March 17, 2019

Ray, my hubby, lover, bff, my pearl, was pronounced deceased at 9:04 am, March 17th, 2019. Ray and I met on the 6th month and the 24th day. He passed away at 64 years old, exactly 6 months and 24 days from his 65th birthday . . .

Interview—each person's perspective.

Carlzbear says ~

"People can be in love, the magnetism that both my parents have as a unit is extremely unique, not only in the black community, but as I have traveled the world, it is unique throughout. I have had the privilege of watching my parents grow up and come together as a unit, the longest of all my siblings. They have instilled in me skill sets that are unteachable and priceless despite my double ivy league degree, which has resulted with the grace of God in my unmerited success."

RayJ (Superman) says ~

A lot is to be said when someone passes and you realize that "you don't know what you got till it's gone." However, I realized my dad's importance way before that. To sum it up, my dad was someone that had so many imperfections, it made him perfect. My childhood was amazing, to say the least. He went to ALL of my games, challenged me when he knew I personally could do better. He was ALWAYS around. Picture this, having such a great childhood that I thought it was the norm for all kids . . . I also thought happiness at Christmas and every birthday and getting everything you wanted was to be expected. Knowing what I know now, the sacrifices both my parents made to make sure we were happy and to give us everything they didn't have was so very commendable. I will always miss my father and will always appreciate what he has done for me as a kid, teenager and young man. "I will forever strive to be the man you were to me and give my kids the childhood they will never realize they had."

LaniBani says ~

My parents had the type the fairy tale love story that most people dream about, but are just not willing to work for. As a young girl I watched their ability to not only accept one another for their faults, but love one another through their faults. A television fairy tale story cannot teach you this. My mom and dad were always honest and driven about who they were, where they came from, and where they wanted to go. Of course, they made mistakes along the way. Those mistakes knocked them down, over, and backwards. However, they always seemed to get up hand in hand, learn from it in prayer, and keep it moving. The lesson I learned is that *I* had to determine who *I* was, where *I* came from and where *I* wanted to go. I then had to find someone who honestly shared that faith and drive with me. When you come from parents like mine, faults are going to be in the one you love . . . Fairy tale love stories are extremely hard work. No one can guarantee that the road will be easy, but what you can determine is that once you find that "**one**", (and you know when you know when you know), with prayer and drive, you WILL make it. How many times you fall is just a minor detail. You keep each other, family, and GOD first. I am blessed to have had a front row seat to this fairy tale love story. I am even more blessed to carry these lessons into my own marriage. THANK YOU MOM & DAD!

Bookyboy says ~

In life, you're only given one Mother and one Father. You can have multiple brothers, sisters, cousins, grandparents, etc., but only one Mom and one Dad. I can honestly say that I have been so blessed with the best two parents I could have ever asked for. Not everyone is given the opportunity to really know their parents, to grow with them, learn from them and even have a close relationship with them. Parents are sacred and are such an instrumental part of your life. My dad especially dedicated so much time and effort to my career and life choices. I'm beyond grateful for his presence. He was a living legend and a major role model in my life and so many others who had the honor to meet him. Throughout my life my dad made so many sacrifices for each and every one one of us and was, and still is, the nucleus of our family. My dad taught me work ethic, responsibility, persistence, loyalty, respect, self-discipline, and best of all, confidence. He taught me confidence in knowing that I will be able to do anything that I put my mind to. He taught me confidence in believing in myself and pursuing whatever I was passionate about. He taught me confidence to keep pushing further and further without any limitations, regardless of how hard life can be sometimes. My father exuded confidence and I looked up to him more than he *probably even knew*. I know he knows that now. I know he is happy and proud of our family as we continue to keep moving forward in honor of him. Ray Anthony Simpson Sr. was, and is, the light of the room. He will forever be the light of my life. Ray, "beam of light," thank you for all that you have done. You have managed to overcome so many obstacles in this life. I am so very proud to call you my dad! I will continue to listen to you in my heart as you continue to guide me in this life, just like you always did . . . Until we meet again Dad, I LOVE YOU.

Vivi says ~

The night Juanita and Ray met was something amazing to witness. It was truly magical from the beginning . . . an unbelievable love story. Two sets of eyes met for the first time all the while knowing that this was the start of an Endless Love . . . The love story of Prince Rayco and Princess Juanita will never be forgotten...

Verdel says ~

If you look at the trajectory of Black love in America, the whole premise is to break us up. Strong Black love is a political statement, we are building, we must focus on our legacy.

Mrs. Virginia A. says ~

As a young boy Ray started out setting goals for his life. He was very impressed with the Real Estate office that was on the corner of Maple Street and Nostrand Avenue that he walked pass every day going to school. He could look through the large glass windows and see the owner, a Black man, dressed in a tailored suit and wearing a shirt and tie. The man did not know Ray or know that Ray was impressed with him and watching him . . . The man, Earl Arrington, and Ray became so close in later years that Ray and his wife called him DAD . . .

ShellyB says ~

279 Kingston Avenue is the iconic address where I met my lifelong friend and neighborhood mentor. Remarkably we both displayed a true enthusiasm for sports and music. When you know someone this long there are many engaging occasions that become way too numerous to recall. However, two happenings have stayed with me: One is the nickname "Sub". Rayco (as we called him) gave me this name relating to a transaction during a sporting event. Two, the night he came by my house to express the ultimate joy he had for his first born, Carla.

No words can express the void, gone but not forgotten . . .

2

Prologue

The story of two youths from Brooklyn who traveled through life together pursuing their dreams. Writing this romantic story has brought me comfort and healing. In the process of writing, I have reconnected with the memories of my soulmate. I wrote these memoirs with God's help. It brought me through so I would be able to minister to someone else through my testimony!!!

My prayer is that in reading our story, all of Rayco's family, friends, loved ones, and anyone who has lost the love of their life, feels less alone. My prayer is that our story helps you to laugh, smile and gain strength, as I did over this journey called grieving.

Thank you so very much for reading my book. You will travel through memory lane with me and by doing so will help me to keep the memory of Rayco alive . . . Thank you again!

3

The Story Begins

Wednesday night, 4/3/19, I envision Ray walking in front of me and his body disintegrating as he passed by. I then saw his face lightly . . . I begin writing this book . . .

A young girl, approximately 18 years old, visits her aunt in Pennsylvania. A friend of her aunt who is a tarot card reader and friend of her aunt decided to read her. The tarot card reader told her that the love of her life will meet her soon. She thought that he was her childhood sweetheart. She said "No." The tarot card reader went on to say that the young girl would have a dream of a young man on a white horse. This would let her know that she will meet the young man soon.

She had the dream . . .

Fast forward one year later after the tarot card reader, I am working at Elaine Powers Health Spa. I am an exercise instructor. I was also a showroom model from time to time and working as a fitness instructor helped me to stay in shape. The modeling career also helped my mom with the rental payments on a home she was renting with an option to buy. A young woman of Panamanian descent approaches me at the health spa. She asks for assistance with the exercise equipment. I assist her. She visits often and consistently asks me for help. A few times, I would ask her if she wanted someone else to help her. She would insist on my helping her . . . One day after several visits, she says "You would be good for my son." I thought she was crazy!

Some time later, posters were circulating about a dinner dance on Fulton Street. I wanted to go. My mom said "No!" I begged. After a while, she said that I could go on one condition. My cousin Vivi had to go with me. We went.

The Story Begins | 15

COUSIN VIVI AND ME

Until now, I didn't realize that was the beginning of my journey.

BROWN SUGAR PRODUCTIONS

ANNUAL

DINNER DANCE

FEATURING

A LIVE BAND

...AND FUNK MASTER SOUNDS

BY

MASTERFLEET

WHEN: FRIDAY, JUNE 24TH

LADIES – DRESS TO IMPRESS! GENTS - $5 AT THE DOOR
(FREE BEFORE 10PM--$3 AFTER)
(FREE BEFORE 12 MIDNIGHT WITH FLYER)

*DOORS OPEN 8–UNTIL   *1264 FULTON (BET BEDFORD & NOSTRAND)

This is a replica of the original flyer. I actually found the original in Rayco's room after his passing, but it was worn and weathered. I replaced the sketched drawing on the flyer of a man and woman dancing to a picture of Ray and me dancing. The address on the flyer is now the site of a Footlocker or some sort of clothing store . . .

Vivi and I drove from Queens to Fulton Street in Bed Stuy, Brooklyn. When we walked into the dinner dance, the band had just finished performing. The DJ, MASTERFLEET, was preparing to mix. I had no idea that the DJ on the flyer, "Masterfleet," was a one man show who went by the name of Ray Anthony Simpson, Sr. By the way, we still have that flyer. I took one look at the DJ and said to my cousin "I am going to marry this guy." My cousin laughed and said "You are crazy." Maybe I was. However, I was determined to make eye contact. When we locked eyes, he asked me to come to the DJ booth. I looked around, questioning, "Me?" I went up to the door of the DJ booth. He asked my name. I told him.

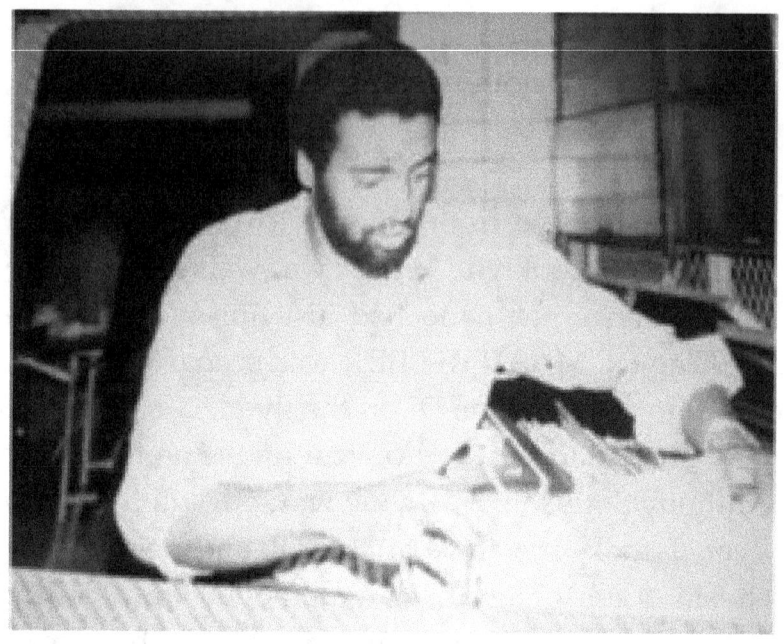

DJ RAYCO

DJ RAYCO

He gave me his name. I raised my hand to shake hands with him, he greeted my hand and kissed my hand gently. I was in awe! We danced that night, intermittently, while he was working. The first song we danced to was "You and I" by Rick James and Tina Marie. The second song we danced to was "Just Keep Me Hanging On" by Ashford and Simpson. Boy, could he dance! When we hustled to "Love Is The Message," every eye was on us . . . Fast forward many years later, we found ourselves sitting behind Ashford and Simpson at a concert . . .

. . .

At the end of the party, he asked me to go to breakfast.

RAYCO AND I AS A YOUNG COUPLE AT HIS SISTER'S BARBECUE

Now, when I was 19, a girl with a mother like mine could not leave a dance and go to breakfast to break curfew, especially with a man. I took him up on his offer. However, the catch was we had to have breakfast at *"my mother's"* house. He agreed. My mother was patiently waiting at the door when we got there, you see I got home pretty late. I introduced Rayco, the name he gave me, to my mother. My mother, this petite, beautiful, Cuban woman, sternly shook his hand and looked deep into his eyes. She allowed him to join us; however, her eyes were on his every move.

MY MOM

After breakfast, Rayco turned to me and said, "Now you should meet my mom." Although many would find this odd, Rayco and I didn't want the night to end. We both just couldn't face the idea of saying "goodbye." Rayco mentioned to his adult children and friends many years later that he forgot to collect his paycheck for that night. I guess meeting me was his "reward!"

I took him up on his offer. Rayco and his mom lived in Crown Heights, Brooklyn. Crown Heights was considered a better neighborhood. I was from Bedford Stuyvesant. Needless to say, I thought that I had met someone less poor than me.

To my *surprise*, as we walked up the stairs to his apartment, I realized that I had *already* met his mother. As I mentioned previously, I worked at Elaine Powers. The young woman of Panamanian descent who had said "You would be good for my son," was Ray's mother. So you can only imagine the *shock* on my face when I saw her.

RAYCO'S MOM

We ate again. We talked. Rayco's mom was so happy to see me!

4

Our Foundation

I want to talk a little about Rayco's mom and my mom. Ms. P (Rayco's mom) was an immigrant from Panama. She was a very hardworking woman who actually helped Rayco's dad, Norman, to come to this country. He was from Jamaica. Ms. P helped many immigrants looking for a better life to come to this country. Ms. P's dad was considered a white Panamanian. He passed away young. Ms. P then brought her mom to the United States.

Ms. P did a lot of the cooking for our children during the early years of Rayco and my marriage. Every morning the house would smell good from some of her favorite dishes like ackee and codfish, callaloo, curry chicken, to name a few. Also, when Carlzbear was born, she never had to see a doctor except for regular visits. Every ailment she had was handled by Ms. P.

Rayco had several bouts with asthma as a child. Ms. P would work long late shifts at the hospital, only to have to return several times with Rayco who was suffering an acute asthma attack. He was always given albuterol as an asthma treatment. It later was found to be a contributing cause to his heart issues . . .

RAYCO, HIS MOM WITH 'SUPERMAN' AND CARLZI

My mom, Grandma C, as the children would call her, was a 2nd generation immigrant from Cuba. She moved in with us when we bought our 2nd home. Rayco had asked her to . . . She helped immensely with raising our children. They are all wonderful adults. I know that this has a lot to do with my mom's dedication to our children. She read the Bible with them. She helped them to do their homework. She didn't do much cooking or knitting, however, as I said previously, Ms. P was there to handle that!

My mom co-owned a nursery with my aunt for single parent moms when I was a young girl. At that time you didn't have to have a license. They just rented an apartment and watched the children in the apartment. I remember coming home from school in Bedford Stuyvesant, Brooklyn. I would complete my homework and then gather all of the nursery school children around a table to help them complete their homework. I loved teaching them and showing them how to complete, especially, their math homework. I always loved math. My philosophy was that in order for my mom and me to succeed and escape poverty, we had to appreciate the value of a dollar.

MY MOM, LANIBANI, 'SUPERMAN', CARLZI AND ME

My grandma and grandpa on my mom's side, were immigrants. My grandmother came directly from Cuba to this country. My grandpa came from Jamaica. However, he was disowned by his family when he married my grandma. My grandma could only speak Spanish, however, she had very dark skin and very long coarse hair. I am mentioning this because in this country my grandma, Irene LaCruz, was considered a Black woman, despite the fact that she was 100% a Cuban native. My grandpa, however, who was a Cuban and Jamaican native, was welcomed into this country due to his fair skin, soft features and fine hair. Only in America!

During the time that we were dating, I recall having an argument with Rayco. You see, we both had trust issues mostly because of our upbringing . . . After having this argument, I was driving and had to get on the Interboro Parkway . . . I had a horrible accident. Rayco was calling my home during the day around the same time. We didn't have cell phones. My mom just kept telling Rayco that I wasn't home until she got a call from the paramedics. I was brought home. My car was totaled. The highlight of the evening, however, was that Rayco walked, took a subway, and the bus to come and see me . . .

Several months later, I was visiting Rayco. He had to go to a DJ gig. I stayed with his mom. You see, he didn't much like me to go to these "underground" parties. A young lady called at Rayco's mom's house. She answered. The young lady asked for Rayco. Ray's mom very abruptly told her, "He's married." I looked at her. I looked at my ring finger. I was confused. She hung up the phone and said "She will not be calling here again!" When I told this to Ray, he simply said "That's my mom for you!"

One day, some six months later, we were at Prospect Park. Rayco dropped to his knees and said "Will you marry me?" I laughed. He frowned and said, "Where would you like to live?" I responded, "Somewhere on Long Island with several kids and a white picket fence." He said, "If you give me a chance, we can do that."

5

Our Worlds Merge

I was a Thoroughbred model. I enjoyed what I did. I remember giving my mom a big check after one of my modeling "catwalk" shows. She used this check to move us out of Brooklyn when I was 17 years old. We moved to Jamaica, Queens.

MY SHOWROOM MODELING

MY SHOWROOM MODELING

MY SHOWROOM MODELING

While we were dating, Rayco was that gentleman who would accompany me to my modeling gigs and just be present. We never crowded each other's space. You could say we totally respected each other's space. Rayco and I were like bookends. When we embarked on a plan, whatever his thoughts were, it was my goal to make it happen, and visa versa. He always had my back and I had his . . .

RAYCO AND I ON OUR HONEYMOON

Approximately three years later, after visiting each other every day, I went to visit Rayco at his apartment that he had recently rented. He wanted to move out from living with his mom. He said to me, "Do you want to go further with this relationship?" I said "Yes, I would like a friendship ring." He said "Okay." Within the next few days, we went to the Diamond District in midtown Manhattan. We travelled by subway. When we entered the store, a nice middle-aged Jewish gentleman asked if he could help us. I asked to see the friendship rings. He looked at Rayco and said, "You want to get this beautiful, young girl a friendship ring?" Ray's face was stoic. He went on to say, "I have many nice, young men in the back who would want to get her an engagement ring." Looking at Ray's face, I was a little concerned at where this conversation could go. I promptly said, "I will be happy with a friendship ring." Ray and I left the jeweler after several hours of price negotiating. I was thrilled! He looked miserable. I also remember Ray limping that day. He was having a problem with his knee after recently falling while playing basketball. That was my Rayco!

Some months later, I remember we were at my mom's home and after eating, Ray asked to speak to my mom. He proceeds to ask my mom for permission to marry me. With her stern, cordial way, she said "Okay." I remember this to be in the fall. Looking back, I am so proud of Rayco. He didn't come from a two-parent household, with a dad who asked his grandmother for permission to marry his mother, yet he knew the honorable thing to do . . . We were married on July 25th.

. . .

Rayco's best man was ShellyB. Everyone called Rayco and Shelly B, "McFadden and Whitehead." Rayco, when performing as a DJ, would always play "Ain't No Stopping Us Now." This is a song by McFadden and Whitehead. It is ironic that the song portrayed everything Rayco and I stood for. ShellyB became our first son's godfather . . . ShellyB has remained Rayco's friend throughout our entire journey.

RAYCO AND SHELLYB

One Valentine's Day, Shelly B, his girl, Rayco and I were going out dancing in Manhattan. We had taken a room in the Penta Hotel, where ShellyB worked. At this time, I didn't drink alcoholic beverages. I remember having several pink champales.

The last thing that I remember was me falling in the tub. I called out to Rayco and said, "Rayco, help, I've fallen. I can't get up." He came to my rescue, however, all of our friends were hysterically laughing.

I want to share a story about ShellyB and Rayco and the dynamics of their friendship . . . A random guy is selling VCRs outside of the Penta Hotel. He and ShellyB talk, and he persuades ShellyB that he can sell them for $300. ShellyB relays this to Rayco. Rayco decides to buy a VCR. You see, Rayco was always interested in electronics. Rayco gives the random guy the money only to find out that the box has no VCR and is stuffed with newspaper. Rayco approaches ShellyB who is mortified! However, Rayco tells him not to worry about it. Rayco says, "I make money, money doesn't make me." Again, an example of Rayco's loyalty as a friend. It was more important to him to have ShellyB as a friend than to worry about the money.

RAYCO, KIM, SHELLYB, HIS SOON-TO-BE WIFE, AND ME

One of my closest friends, as pictured above, gave me my first birthday party. She is still my friend, and also became Carlzbear's godmother . . . It was my 21st birthday party. I remember that I wasn't speaking to Rayco during the time. She, however, invited Rayco to the party. When I walked into her home, I saw Rayco who appeared to be having a good time with "someone of the female persuasion." Needless to say, I started talking to "someone of the male persuasion." By the end of the evening, Rayco and I were in each other's arms . . .

Less than two years later, we got married. We didn't

have the lavish wedding many young people have today. We were married at St Alban's Congregational Church. Rayco's sister hosted the reception in her backyard. This is a tradition for people of Island ancestry and, in our case, we were a couple who needed to count their pennies (smile). Our wedding dance was to Lionel Richie and Diana Ross' "Endless Love." I am still brought to tears when I hear this song. We lived with my mom until the fall of that same year when we bought our first home in Hillside, Queens. Life was good.

1st HOUSE

6

Children Arrive

February 19th, we had our first child at 7 pounds, 11 ounces. I was born on the 7th. Rayco was born on the 11th. We still tease her to this day, saying she possibly could be the owner of the "7-Eleven Stores." An interesting course of events happened during this time. We had purchased a car from Potamkin Cadillac in Manhattan. The salesperson's name was Tom Tedesco. We inadvertently, being a young pregnant couple, left the paperwork at the dealership. On the night that I was delivering our first child, our Fleetwood Brougham Cadillac was stolen.

I called Potamkin for the paperwork after I was released from the hospital. They said the salesman no longer worked there. Also, they didn't have any paperwork. When GMAC called and sent invoices for the car payment, I then called GMAC and told them that the car was stolen. In so many words, they confirmed that this was my problem. We decided to get an attorney. Our attorney ended up becoming disbarred. Rayco would always comment that some ethnic groups work harder than others. I won't comment on what ethnicity this attorney was; but yes, he was disbarred. I had taken some legal classes in college. I took a test and became a Certified Paralegal and Notary. It took some time, however, we won the case. Rayco and I did it again. The lien was paid and we won money for pain and suffering. This is how Rayco and I operated. We were ride or die for each other.

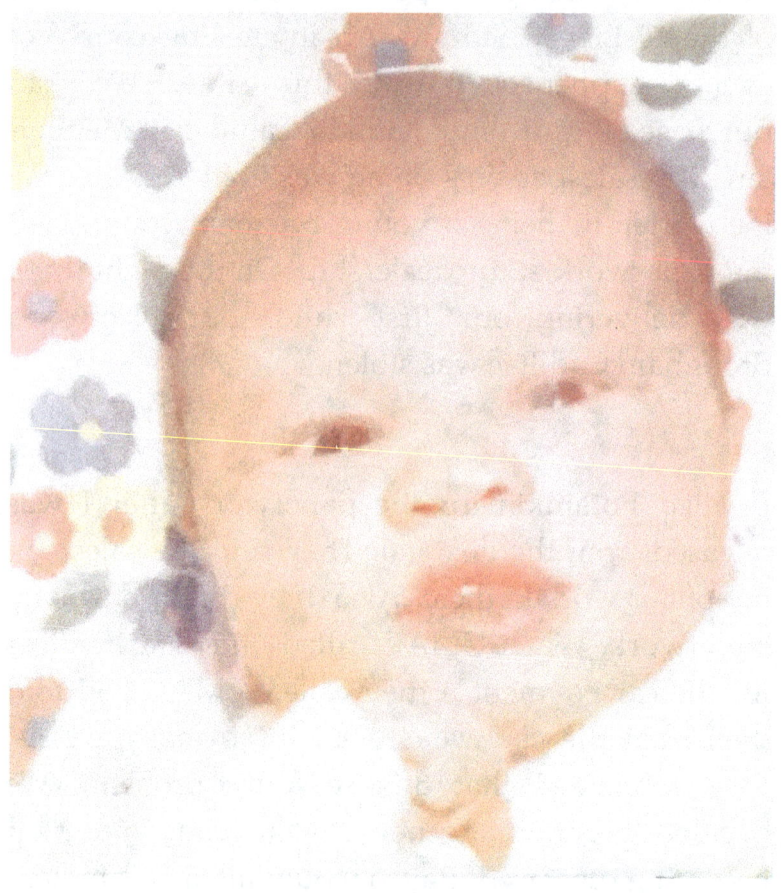

1ST PIC OF CARLZI

Children Arrive | 49

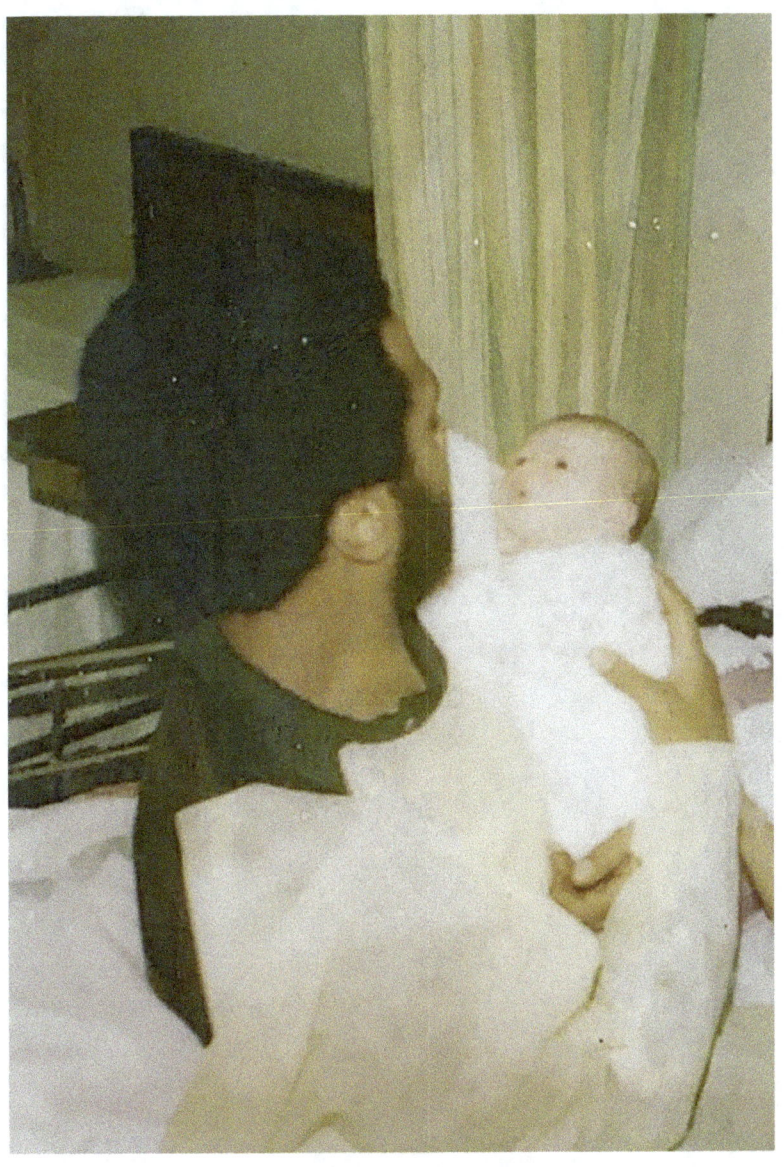

1ST PIC OF CARLZI AND RAYCO

OUR CARLZI

CARLZI AND ME

Our first daughter was the apple of our eye. I named our first born after one of my closest friends who was my friend since childhood. As I previously said, she is my friend to this day. She is the one who gave me my 21st birthday. She came over one day and smelled the baby. She asked, "Have you washed her?" I said "No, I don't know how." We proceeded to wash the one-month old baby in my bathroom sink.

. . .

Carlzbear, or "Vanilla Pudding" as Rayco nicknamed her, is such a blessing! She was on a Luvs baby commercial as a very young baby. She was the only baby that wasn't crying during the taping. I stood on the side. As long as she saw me, she smiled constantly. On her first visit to the doctor, I remember this doctor saying when you have a baby like her, you should have many more!

When Carlzbear was three, I delivered our first boy. We had named him Ray J, after Rayco. Ray J was a tremendous baby. To date, he was my biggest birth. :) On the day I delivered him, I went into shock. My husband yelled at the doctors asking, "Is she going to be okay?" My body was trembling all over, but I loved the size and look of my newborn baby boy. Rayco's name for him was "Superman!"

Rayco proceeded to call his best friend, ShellyB. The two of them went to Coney Island to celebrate. Now, with my first, I nursed her for four months. RayJ, however, after two weeks, looked at me as if to say "Are you planning to feed me with *your* body?" I am on the slim side. I therefore made him some Karo syrup, corn meal cereal and Carnation Milk. Ms. P taught me the recipe. He was over 30 pounds in one year.

RAY J

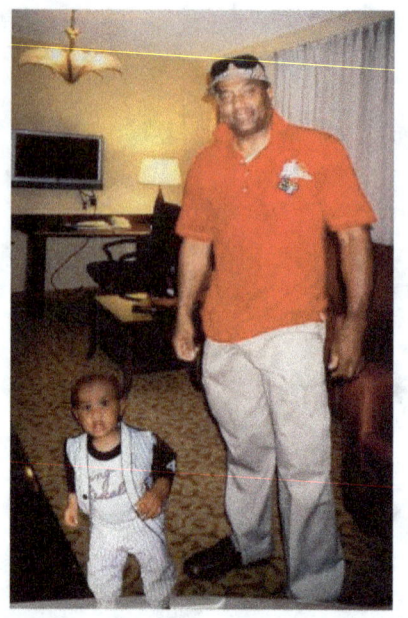

RAY J BEGINNING TO WALK WITH DAD BY HIS SIDE

RayJ looks older than he is. He is actually just shy of 12 months at this time.

Children Arrive | 55

'SUPERMAN' AND ME

RayJ, as I mentioned, was very large. When he was two years old, Rayco and I wanted to take the three children to DisneyWorld in Orlando, Florida. Rayco reached out to his only sister, and she was able to secure discounted tickets so we would be able to afford the visit. RayJ by now was well over 60 pounds. At that time, children 3 and under were allowed free entry into DisneyWorld. RayJ, however, was huge. Rayco was physically holding RayJ in an effort to show he was under three. When we got to the admitting line, no one believed us. Thank God, I brought his birth certificate, which I literally traveled with, so that we could prove that our baby RayJ, was under three years old. I will NEVER forget this.

 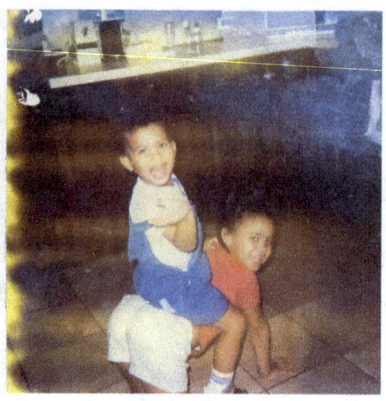

CARLZI AND RAYJ HAVING FUN

7

Long Island

Now, after RayJ was born, we had decided to move to Long Island. We hosted many "pay" parties to raise money for the move. At one party, I asked everyone to bring a bottle. Rayco or I collected the bottles as each person arrived. However, when the guests went to the make-shift bar for a drink, they were charged for each drink. Rayco's friends, one by one, went to him and said, "Your wife is charging me for a glass from the bottle I bought." Rayco said, "That's my girl." Eventually, I stopped. However, it became another conversation with Rayco and his friends.

We went on an active search. The first house we found, I had originally gone to see alone with the broker. I loved it so much that I wanted to come back to show my husband. When I arrived to the home, we walked up the driveway and knocked on the door. No one answered, but a curtain moved. We went to the nearest outdoor phone to call the broker. Outdoor phones were the way to contact people at that time. There were no cell phones . . . To my surprise, she said, "The owner JUST took the house off the market." I was disappointed; however, I knew in the back of my mind what had happened. It is very "interesting" living on Long Island as an ethnic person . . .

· · ·

We renewed our search for a home. I found another home, with plenty of property and trees. I loved it more than the first property. I went back to visit with my mom. The owner fell in love with my mom. He would cut fresh roses for her every time we visited. I had a good feeling about this house.

OLD BACKYARD BEFORE THE POOL

The day we closed on the house, Rayco was laid off from his job. He called around to business contacts to see if someone would hire him. As a result, one of his contacts said that he would hire him as a subcontractor. Ray obliged. He went to Riverhead and applied for a tax ID number. He was extremely late for the closing. However, this occurrence resulted in the birth of "Simpco Cable Company." This is the man Rayco was—determined, focused, and with one goal above all others, to take care of his family.

We both were raised in apartments, living on the 2nd floor in tenement housing. For a period of time, my mom and I lived in the projects. At one time my mom and I had to share the use of a bathroom with everyone on the same floor. Sometimes one of the men from one of the families would literally peak and watch me while I was in the bathroom. It was absolutely disgusting.

It was such a blessing to close on a home that we could call our own!

When Rayco was just a 9-year-old boy, he asked the owner of the deli down the block for a job. When asked why, he answered, "My mom is sick."

We moved into our "dream home" on Long Island. The night we moved in, it was pouring rain. The skylight in the dining room was leaking. We moved in with the help of Rayco's friends. So as we stepped in puddles, yes, inside the house, one of Rayco's friends said he was hungry. They all chimed in. I was elected to go to the nearest store around the corner for food. Rayco and I moved into our suburban area in the mid-1980s. However, at that time, I never really gave it a thought on how society was, and sometimes still is. I walked into Waldbaum's, shopping for cold cuts, etc. I gradually began to notice everyone looking at me. After I paid for my snack food and began to walk out of the store, an older man pulled his cart next to me and asked very abruptly "What are you doing here?" I answered, also very abruptly, "The same thing that you are doing here . . . at the store!" I then walked off and put my groceries and myself into the car and drove off. I told everyone when I got back to our new home. Years later, it became a story we always told our friends. Again, welcome to Long Island!

We moved in with our two children, our girl, a little over 3 years old and our first-born son, 7 months old.

On the second day of living into our new home. Our Carlzbear decided she wanted to explore her surroundings. We owned a male Doberman. His name was King. King loved Carlzbear and would follow her anyplace she went. She walked and walked until she found herself in the next cul-de-sac. King was right by her side.

KING

She was in the backyard of another home. The residents tried to come out to talk to our three and a half year old to try and find out where she came from. At every attempt they made trying to come outside, King would greet them with a harsh growl.

At the same time, I was trying to call the nearby police and report my child missing. The police detective had asked for a description of the child. I described her as she is—namely, a fair skinned Black little girl with light eyes and two pigtails. After some time, the police called back and asked, "Could she be described as Hispanic or Italian?" I said, "Yes." We found Carlzbear. Our new neighbors offered to drive Rayco around the block so that he could retrieve his child. When he returned, he let me know that the residents at the home thought that the neighbor was Carlzbear's father. Rayco told me that he politely corrected them!

8

More On The Way

Several years later, we had another baby girl. I remember one of Rayco's closest friends asking "Another one?" During the pregnancy of my first two children—and even my last—I could feel if each was a boy or girl. I was correct with both. During my third pregnancy, with our second baby *girl,* all during the pregnancy, I thought that she was a boy. I had several boy's names to choose from.

My mother-in-law moved to Florida some years after our marriage. However, she would always travel from Florida to Long Island to assist me, along with my mother, with all of my deliveries.

When I went into labor, I remember walking around our circular driveway with my mother-in-law. My mom stayed inside, as it was hard for her to see me in labor. I went over some of the male names with my mother-in-law. She said, "What if the baby is a girl?" I said, "With all of the kicks and movement inside of my stomach, I really believe the baby is a boy." I went on to say, "I have been correct with each of my other predictions." She said, "Well, if it happens to be a girl, I saw a beautiful Hawaiian name in this magazine that I was reading." Needless to say, I had to use the Hawaiian-based name. I changed the spelling so as to make the name sound more ethnic.

This was Rayco's baby. As she took her first breath, she only wanted daddy. Mom, me, was only good for nursing in the beginning . . .

Approximately one year after her birth, I took an evening word processing job to help make ends meet. When I would come home late at night, "Stinky phat pudding" or "Lani Bani" as her dad had named her, would be in the bed with her dad. As I tried to snuggle into bed, she would literally push me away. If Rayco or I would put her in her crib, she would proceed to cry all night! Looking back, I must say that I love her persistence! She is now Lead Counsel at a major firm. Go figure . . .

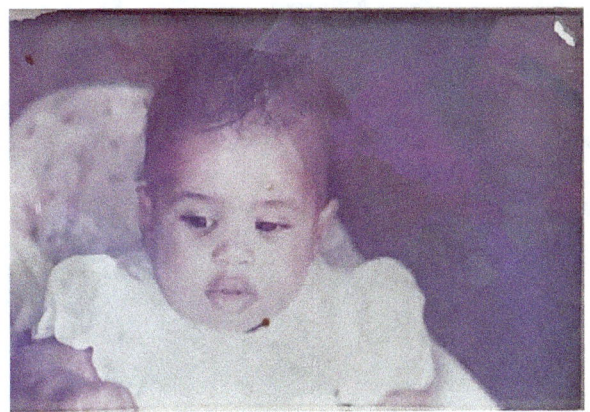

LANIBANI

LANIBANI, aka 'STINKY PUDDINGS,' AND ME

STINKY PUDDINGS WITH HER DAD

Ms. LaniBani, as previously mentioned, is a very determined spirit . . . She decided in high school that she wanted a Step Team at her non-ethnic school district. She asked me to accompany her to a Board meeting. When the Board opened the floor for community resident questions and/or requests, she stood up to request that she be able to start a Step Team. The Board thought she meant an "Irish Step Dancing Team." How funny. She very politely said, "No, I mean a traditional African-American

Step Team." After winning approval, she then asked the principal if her mom could be the advisor.

I also remember taking her back and forth to Weehawken, New Jersey. She was a fitting model for many years . . . She also followed her mom in the field of modeling.

LANIBANI MODELING

We now had three kids. On a side note, when we were looking at homes, I often asked my mom to go along. Ray was often times working. When we found our "Dream Home," Rayco asked my mom to move in with us. I don't know if he asked her because he knew that my mom and I were inseparable or because he had the foresight to know we would need a babysitter. Both reasons would be correct. My mom was my right-hand person with the children. Because of her and the many visits from Grandma P, Rayco's mom, our children were never taken care of by a babysitter.

Rayco had several jobs to take care of his family. On one occasion, he had a Lincoln Continental. He was an "Uber" driver before there were Uber Drivers. He took all of us out driving. The car broke down. It was pouring rain outside. Rayco, the kind of man he was, constantly worked on the car. He then took a container and walked to the gas station. He walked back and forth. No one stopped to help. "Carlzbear," our first born daughter, and I were in the back seat. After many cold and rainy hours, Rayco got the car started. He got us home safely . . . After this incident, every time it was raining, Rayco would say, "It's raining Ray" . . . This would indicate it was a good day . . . .

After our third child was born, money was even tighter. We had three children and one income. As stated previously, I decided to try to work. I worked as an evening word processor at Underwriters Laboratories. After working there for some time and speaking with other couples, I came home and said to Rayco that we should adopt a son. He asked me why? I said, "Because there are so many ethnic children who need homes. I want to help. Also, Ray Jr. needs a playmate." I had spoken to a friend of mine who gave me a number to call. I set up an appointment to go. I had a doctor's appointment on the same day. Ray and I were to first go to the doctor's office and then to the adoption office appointment.

Dr. Asher gave me an examination and said, "Guess what? You are pregnant." I looked at Ray. Needless to say, we never made it to the adoption office. After nine months, we introduced our fourth child, our baby boy, to the world.

1ST PIC OF JON

FUTURE J5 WITH MOM

LANI AND BOOKYBOY . . . ALL OF THEM ARE VERY CLOSE

Rayco nicknamed our 4th child, BookyBoy. He was, and will always be, mom's baby. When BookyBoy was about 4 years old, Weslyann, the pre-school all of our children attended, was taking the students on a trip. Rayco had, as mentioned, his Simpco Cable business. I was the secretary, payroll, etc. I asked one of the moms of another student to please pick up our son, and take him with her son on the trip. Some hours later, I received a call asking why I left our son home today from the trip. I replied, "He did go on the trip." I abruptly left my "shift" with Simpco Cable, and went to the park where the students were. I did not see our son. I was panicking. After several hours, a very polite older gentleman came over to me and asked me if I was looking for my son. I said, "Yes." He then said that my son had been playing with his grandson and he didn't know where the parents were. He then took my son to the nearby precinct, hoping someone would come and claim him. I hurried to the nearby precinct and saw BookyBoy on the counter, eating candy, laughing and having a good time with the police officers. I knew from that day on that J5 would be fine in any situation and throughout his life!

By the time Rayco and I had our 4th, we had "perfected" the parenting game. One "look" and our children knew we meant business. They could not as easily put one parent against the other. Money was sooo tight, though. Looking back, there were many arguments. However, one thing always remained the same. I felt like I would not be able to breathe without Rayco in my life, hence my writing this book. This book is my way of keeping Rayco and our love affair alive!

• • •

Rayco had a name for each of his children. RayJ's name, as I wrote, was "Superman." When our Superman was two, just after I had birthed our third, he was taken to the hospital for bronchial asthma. He was extremely thin. Rayco and I worried for RayJ's life. I would go and visit him with our baby girl. I would nurse her, while looking at and singing to RayJ. Rayco came to the hospital and presented RayJ with his first doll. It was the ALF doll. I remember RayJ and his father smiling. RayJ has that ALF doll to this day. As a matter of fact, it currently sits in his first child's, my 2nd granddaughter's bedroom.

'SUPERMAN' WITH BOOKYBOY AND LANIBANI

9

The "Manor"

The first five years living at the "Manor" as Rayco would describe it in the early years, were financially difficult. Rayco's friends would call us the modern day "Bonnie & Clyde". Within the nine years living there, all four children were born. My mom and I would shovel the snow in the winter. We would attempt to take care of the lawn in the spring. Rayco worked at least two jobs. Despite the arguments over money, one thing remained clear. I needed him in my life and he would always say he needed me.

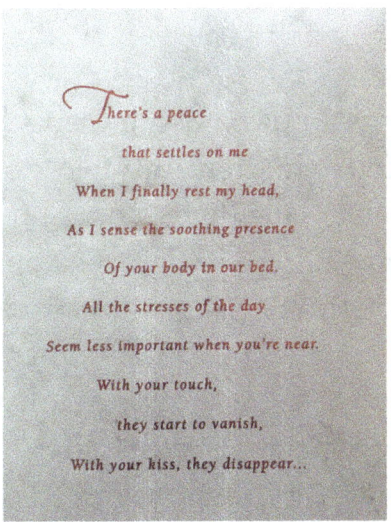

There's a peace
that settles on me
When I finally rest my head,
As I sense the soothing presence
Of your body in our bed,
All the stresses of the day
Seem less important when you're near.
With your touch,
they start to vanish,
With your kiss, they disappear...

VERSE FROM CARD I GAVE RAYCO IN 2007

Rayco, after working each and every day, would attempt to take care of my world. He would make me, my mom, and the four children safe by quietly fixing, renewing, or replacing what needed to be done. In my current state of mind, busy taking care of the kids, if I remembered to turn anything on, I would usually forget to disconnect it or turn it off. I took for granted that what needed to run, sprinkle or turn off, would do so on its own. I remember Rayco, later in his life, calling me "lights on."

Many times I invited Ms. P, Rayco's mom, to visit. On her first visit, I remember her saying, "Now this is a home!"

What made our house a home to me, however, was having the four children, the two dobermans and later rottweillers, the two moms—namely, Ms. P and my mom— along with Rayco and myself. We were the American dream. It was exactly what I had told him that I wanted when we walked together in Prospect Park. All my Rayco wanted . . . was me! I learned many years later that he would have foregone everything, to have me by his side. He worked day and night, at his job and kept up with the house, to make me happy. *I* was his "American dream." He would say "You know that you are married to the Pearl." I always laughed at that. However, Rayco was . . . is my Pearl. The day before he took his last breath, I told him that . . . He was my soulmate!

It is important to also note that Rayco and I came from single-parent households. I, a woman, was raised by a remarkable mother. On many nights she and I slept on the floor and made it a very comfortable bed. Many times rodents would pass by our feet. I was so tired from all of the after-school activities my mom had me in that I didn't even care. My mom, the rodents, and I all slept well . . . She taught me to be confident, determined, and a God-fearing woman. Rayco, was also raised by a remarkable woman. She taught him to take care of himself and ultimately his family. Rayco's father was absent from his life. Rayco was raised without a father's direction and guidance. I am sure Rayco's dad had his own struggles as he was an immigrant from Jamaica. Therefore, Rayco had to basically teach himself to be a man . . . later, a husband and father!

RAYCO'S DAD, NORMAN SIMPSON WITH RAYCO

MY DAD, ROBERT CANTY

My father passed away when I was 12. My father was in the army and received an honorable discharge at a very young age. He suffered from sickle cell anemia. His folded flag presented to the family at his passing is still on our fireplace mantle.

We were both raised in extremely poor households. I remember Rayco and my mom comparing how poor each of them was growing up. My mom always won the comparison, though I am not sure if that is a comparison one would want to win!

Despite the financial and emotional hardship of our upbringing, we were determined to persevere. We both struggled with emotional hurts, strongholds and demons from our past that presented themselves from time to time throughout our marriage. When bad things happen to you as a child, you feel as though it's your fault. These events help shape a lot of your personality, good or bad, as an adult. Our marriage, our covenant, nonetheless, always prevailed. God blessed our union!

10

Simpco Cable Company

*A*s previously mentioned, Simpco Cable Company, was born out of necessity. Rayco was a sole proprietor. I was the beneficiary, the secretary, confidante, lover, and anything else he needed to get him through the day. I called Ray, Rayco. I really don't know when I started calling him this. However, the root of the name is from Ray and Simpco . . .

Rayco took all of his employees, three to be exact, out to dinner at Peter Luger's Steak House after his first big contract. I was pregnant with RayJ at the time . . . The steak was good but all I can remember is that I asked everyone for their portion of the creamed spinach..I loved the creamed spinach. Rayco was shocked that I could eat so much. After RayJ was born, he understood why . . .

One hot and sunny day we were driving to Brooklyn for one of Rayco's subcontracting jobs. We drove into a pretty rough neighborhood. Rayco decided to pass by the block where I grew up. I want to mention that neighborhood now has $1 million plus homes. Two of our four children, Carlz, 10, and RayJ, approximately 7 years old, were in the back seat. As we drove down the block, windows open, Rayco said, "Hey guys, this is where your mom grew up." Carlz responds and said, "Dad, can we please close the windows?" It was then that Rayco and I concluded our children will definitely appreciate a different lifestyle from what we were afforded.

Rayco worked two to three jobs from time to time. He worked for many companies, including Honeywell Inc. It was there that Rayco met Peter O, who worked side by side with him. Peter O told me that he and Rayco would go out for lunch together. It was during this time that they would sometimes work out at Bally's Gym. It was bought by LA Fitness many years later. Sometimes they would play basketball during lunch. Sometimes they would just go to Red Lobster, Rayco's favorite restaurant, to eat and drink. Rayco asked Peter O to be LaniBani's godfather when she was born. He really appreciated his friendship with Peter O!

As previously mentioned, he also had his businesses. He started with Simpco Cable Company. Several years later he started another business, Point To Point Communications. He was the sole proprietor of both. He also had a car service, along with his regular 9am to 5pm jobs.

• • •

Rayco's dad was an entrepreneur. He dabbled a lot in real estate. However, as previously mentioned, he was absent from Rayco's years as a young boy. Rayco still tried to follow in the footsteps of his dad. Later in life, he also did some dabbling in real estate. Rayco also was able as a young man to identify the successful businessmen who owned and operated their offices and stores in the community. One man, who shall be discussed later in the book, stood out to Rayco . . .

Every time there was a car accident where someone hit our car or hurt us in some way, Rayco would say, "We need to see an attorney." He would then want to invest in something. He would always say, "Cars depreciate, let's invest in something that would benefit our future." We had several occasions early in our marriage when we did purchase a car. The first time was when we won our court case against GMAC. We purchased a Peugeot. Rayco, after a while, called the car a Peush-- . . . I don't even think these cars are on the road now . . .

If someone did wrong by the family, he would definitely seek counsel to get to the bottom of it and use that for the family's benefit.

I again attempted to help him out. I looked into the want-ad section of *Newsday*. I saw a position that was available and that I thought would be good for me to do at home. It was a home news transcriber. I told Rayco about it. He said that I needed a computer to do this job. Within a few days, Rayco came home with a computer. I started my business as a home news monitor. I did this for several years. My mom helped with the kids while I would be locked in my room transcribing news reports on my computer.

My mom was so very helpful, like I said earlier. She was my right-hand person. When Rayco and I married. I promised her that I would complete college. I had dropped out to marry Rayco. So I decided, while I was home working as a home news monitor, to take full advantage of the time. I re-enrolled in college. When I started, BookyBoy was very young. I was still in college when Carlz entered high school. On one of the many occasions that I visited the high school, this particular day the principal at the time walked up to me. He said, "You are here so much, why don't you pursue education?" This was the beginning of my pursuit into the field of education. He even donated some of his "staff" letters. (A staff letter is a type of compensation given to educators and is presented in the form of college credits.) A few years later, I became a teacher.

I want to again mention Rayco was a DJ. He was, in fact, one of the first disc jockeys who spun records at the very *first* West Indian Day parade in Brooklyn, some 45 years ago.

His closest nephew, as Rayco would say, told me that he would love to spin records on Rayco's equipment when he was young. Mike, Rayco's nephew, tells the story that in the early 1970s, Rayco was the DJ who would always spin records on the corner of Eastern Parkway and Kingston Avenue every Labor Day. He would have a wall of speakers behind him. One year, Rayco gave Mike some business cards to pass out. On the card was a picture of a huge sail ship and it said Masterfleet III. Mike kept one of the cards and took it to school to brag about his uncle who had the wall of speakers on the corner of Eastern Parkway and Kingston Avenue.

. . .

One particular story that Mike, Rayco's nephew, tells is one that truly embodies Rayco and his drive . . . One Saturday when Mike was about 4 or 5 years old, Ray came home from playing football with his uniform on. Mike asked him if he had won. He also said that he wished he was able to see his game. Rayco said to him, "Of course I won. If you don't believe me, watch." He then turned on the T.V. and a football game was on. Rayco said to Mike, "Look, can't you see me?" He showed Mike a player with the same white jersey and black number that he had on. Now, Mike says, thinking about it, he isn't sure if the number was really black—it could have been green, brown or red, because the televisions at that time were only black and white. They watched the rest of the game and Mike remembers cheering everytime #36 ran with the ball, thinking all the time that it was his uncle Rayco. Mike says even to this day, he will cheer for the team with a white jersey and black numbers.

Simpco Cable Company | 97

MIKE AND RAYCO

Ms. P, Rayco's mom, would say, "Anything that my son touches will turn to gold." He has helped me, notwithstanding God, my mom and dad, to be the confident woman I am today. I have tried to instill that confidence in my daughters. I will try to instill the confidence in my granddaughters and grandsons for as long as God keeps me here. This book is my way of keeping our memory and legacy alive for our children, their children, and so on and so forth!

Now without getting too personal, I would like to share a funny story. As you already have read, we have four children by now. One day, Rayco and I were driving around in Brookville, Long Island. We had just picked up a new car. Rayco was definitely a car fanatic. Rayco proposed that we drive to a wooded area in Brookville to "christen" our new car. Of course, I had to take him up on his challenge. He drove around and found a deserted, woody area. He pulled over and stopped the engine. I chicken out. Rayco started the engine and drove home. When we pulled into the garage, he looked over and said "You are a chicken, but I still love you." I was so happy to hear that. I thought he was disappointed. Maybe he was, but he wasn't going to give me the satisfaction of knowing that.

11

Concerts

*R*ayco and I frequented many concerts together. We have seen Diana Ross, Beyonce, Alicia Keyes, Anita Baker, and Sade, to name a few. One of his favorite comedians was Dave Chappell. Carlz had given us tickets to his show one time. Ray laughed so hard during the concert, he was practically crying. I found his comedy a little "rough around the edges." The comedian spoke of his dad and told the audience that he had told his dad that he didn't like being poor. He went on the say his dad responded that "being poor is a state of mentality. They were simply broke." This touched Rayco. Sometimes when a child is raised a certain way, for instance, like being poor, they never can get this out of their head. They always feel if they stop working for a minute, there is a chance, they could end up the same way they were as a child, poor . . . This was one of Rayco's and my demons . . .

The very first concert we went to was Prince. We were barely out of our teenage years. I'll never forget when he was introducing his band. One person got up and asked, "How would you introduce yourself?" He responded, "I am your mother's favorite freak!" I will never forget that. Rayco took me to see Barry White after I graduated with my first Master's Degree. He was so very proud of me. I am the first in our immediate family to have an Associate's, Bachelor's and Master's Degree.

Barry White was my musical icon. When Rayco and I were dating, I would be in the attic of the house my mom rented. I would play "I Belong To You" over and over again. It was a song sung by Barry White and the Love Unlimited Orchestra.

One one occasion, Ray and I were in the attic in a very compromising position, if you know what I mean . . . I did not hear my mom coming up the stairs, because "I Belong To You" was playing. My mom said "Nita" in a very stern voice. Rayco and I both froze. Mom and I locked eyes. I was humiliated. I am sure that Rayco was too. I then said, "I guess now you have to marry me." Rayco said, "I already proposed to you at Prospect Park. You are the one who laughed, remember?"

So you can only imagine how happy I was to go to Jones Beach to see Barry White live after I had graduated with my Bachelor's Degree many years later. All of the young girls were running to the stage to shake Barry White's hand, after he offered for them to do so. Rayco looks over to me and said, 'If you want, you can go and shake his hand . . . " Before he finished his sentence, I had thrown my pocketbook into his lap, stepped on his and everyone else in the aisle's feet, and made my way up to shake Barry White's hand. Barry said, "You have beautiful eyes!" Of course, Rayco had said that many times. I came back to tell Rayco what he said. He responded, "Wow, now that Barry White has said it, you believe it?"

Rayco's best friend, ShellyB, invited us to see Tina Marie with him and his wife. This was an exceptional concert because as I previously said, our first dance was to "You and I" by Rick James and Tina Marie. I was so happy that Rayco and I got a chance to see Tina Marie. I thank ShellyB for inviting us. Shortly after, Tina Marie passed away at 50 years old. So glad we got a chance to see her. Rick James had already passed away, also at 50 years old . . .

We took all four children to the Thanksgiving Day parade when Jon was very young. I remember that he was still nursing and eating Gerber baby food. This is when we saw Patti LaBelle. She was on a huge float. Rayco called out to her and this time he received the accolades. She saw Rayco as we were right on the curb in front of the crowd. She yelled, "I see you, handsome!" This made Rayco's day, aside from carrying baby bags and trying to keep up with four small children and a wife. Patti saved the day!

RAYCO MODELING AT CARLZI AND LANIBANI FASHION SHOW . . . HE MADE A SPECIAL APPEARANCE

12

A Village ...

As previously mentioned, Rayco and I have had several friends who have come and gone throughout our marriage. We also have extended family that we have met and lost throughout the years. I must mention that my cousin, Vivi, and Rayco's friend, ShellyB, were in our lives before we met, after we met, throughout our marriage. Both check up on me to this day. I will love both of them for as long as I live. I have another friend who must be mentioned. I met her while she was married to one of my estranged cousins. They are now divorced. Several years after she lost her mother, I asked her to bring her father to meet my mom. At first she declined. I was persistent. I have been called that by Rayco many times. She decided to bring her father over for one of our Thanksgiving dinner celebrations. When my mother saw her father, I knew that there was a connection.

My mom was soo happy. Our kids by now were near teen years. Nonetheless, my mom made sure not to show any signs of personal affection in front of the kids. But, I knew my mom. She was in love. She was a very happy 68-69 year old woman, who had an impeccable shape. My mom dated my friend's dad for several years. On my mom's seventy-fifth birthday, I decided to give her a surprise brunch on a boat. I invited him. Rayco and I were diligent in keeping it a secret that he was invited. The lunch cruise was in New York City. My mom had never been on ANY cruise. So this was very important. On the way to Manhattan, my mom was constantly asking Rayco and me why are we going so far?? She wanted to stay local. I kept telling her that all cruises usually leave from New York City. That is still usually the case, however, now there are some cruises that leave from Brooklyn and the Hamptons. My mom continued to question us the entire ride to New York City. When we parked, I immediately spotted her friend. I turned my mom around so that she would *not* see him. She started complaining and saying, "You two didn't have to bring me here." I said, "Rayco and I think you will enjoy this birthday lunch cruise." I motioned my mom to turn around and see the boats. She turned around and saw her friend, Ben. I still remember the happy, shocked, thrilled and loving look on her face. That face was one of the happiest faces I had seen of my mom. I was soo happy Rayco and I had put this together. Three months later, Ben passed away. Three years later, my mom passed away.

BEN AND MOM

One day, in the late 1990's Rayco and I were driving with our baby son in the back seat. A drunk driver hit us head on. Thank God our son was in a car seat. We won a court case after a long and tiring battle.

During this time and before, I had been traveling to and from the East End with a group of friends. We traveled there on many occasions. We would have parties by the water. We had about 10 to 12 children amongst us. The kids would play while we would also "play."

When Rayco and I won the court case, we had to decide on what to invest in. The decision was between a car and another home. Rayco, as previously mentioned, didn't like how cars depreciated so rapidly. We decided to invest in another home. We were one of the youngest couples at the time to get a home in this particular area of the East End. We were welcomed with open arms. We were invited to a Labor Day function given by the neighborhood association. I remember that a photographer from "Dan's Papers" was there. He took many pictures of Rayco and me. Rayco began to say that he recognizes one of the long-term residents. He said, "That's the man. That's the man. I know him!" I asked, "How?" He told me of the story of a young African-American broker who always walked past his apartment with his briefcase, fancy suit, expensive shoes with matching accessories. Rayco said he would always drive off in a big fancy car. Rayco was so impressed by this because as a young boy he had not seen this before. Now, we were on the East End and saw the same man at a social function.

EARL A.

MR. ARRINGTON'S OFFICE WHERE RAYCO SAW HIM GO EVERY DAY. RAYCO WAS VERY PROUD TO KNOW HIM!

I asked Rayco to approach the gentleman and let him know that he knows him. At first Rayco said, "No." He didn't want to disturb the man who was enjoying his family and the party. After some convincing, Rayco approached Mr. Arrington. He told him the story and how he had admired him for many years. After hearing this, he invited Rayco and me to his table. We accepted. We had a wonderful time that night. Not long after, Mr. Arrington and his wife were celebrating their 40th wedding anniversary. He invited us. He asked Rayco to tell the story to all of the invited guests. Everyone was so impressed by Rayco's humility, demeanor and soft spoken, yet, direct approach, in telling his story. However, that was my Rayco . . . my Pearl!

• • •

Rayco wanted everyone to realize the impression this young African American broker had on him as a young boy who was raised by a single mom with no dad on site. Rayco even spoke to me several times about his basketball coach who was tough on him. He said he would tell Rayco that he was too thin or not fast enough. Rayco eventually joined track in determination to increase his speed. He also would say that track helped his legs look bigger...

Rayco sought guidance from people like Mr. Arrington, Mr. Vernon Burrows, and Mr. Barrett. They were three black men who took care of their wives, children and overall families. Rayco later in life sought mentorship from Mr. Arrington on a regular basis. Mr. Arrington was very impressed with Rayco's positive energy and drive. He became very encouraging and supportive to Rayco and his endeavours. These men helped my Rayco to develop into the young determined, hard working and family-orientated man that he was. It has been said many times, It takes a village...

This East End neighborhood is made up primarily of ethnic residents. The neighborhood where we raised our kids and where they went to school is not. It was important to us that our children also see successful ethnic men and women. We didn't want them to think we were the only ethnic people in the world. Two of them, while very young, actually did think our family and the "Cosby Show" family were the only ethnic families in the world. However, the way we raised our adult children, despite the world's prejudices, is a testament to how we view the world!

IT IS IMPORTANT TO NOTE THAT OUR EAST END NEIGHBORHOOD HAS CURRENTLY BEEN RECOGNIZED AS A NEW YORK STATE HISTORICAL LANDMARK . . . THE FACT THAT IT IS FOUNDED BY AFRICAN AMERICANS WITH A DEEP RICH HISTORY HAS PUT OUR EAST END NEIGHBORHOOD ON THE MAP!

Rayco was a dedicated and devoted employee to his job as well. So much so that he was put in the Presidential Club status. His current manager was the one who nominated him and recently told me that when he nominated Rayco, he had been asked to nominate anyone who in his opinion went above and beyond. He wanted to nominate someone who tried to make a difference. Rayco's manager recently said to me, "Simpco would never say 'no' to a job. His work ethic was beyond incredible. He was always available, willing and able to get the job done." To this day, his manager says "I don't know how he was so loyal to the job and yet able to raise such a fine family . . . he believes it is a testament to me and the bond Simpco and I had!"

The particular year that he was put in that status, 2010, we were invited to go to the Dominican Republic. We were picked up by a limo, taken to the airport and were flown business class. We stayed at a 5-star resort for a week. When we landed in the Dominican Republic, I remember saying to Rayco that I felt that I had died and gone to Heaven. He smiled. We had to wear all white on the night that he was honored. Rayco was among ten employees being inducted into the President's Club. This is a club which was exclusively held for the top salesmen of the company. He was the only Communications Technician. He was also the only ethnic! As said all throughout this book, that was my Rayco!

PRESIDENTIAL CLUB PLAQUE

It is important to note that on Rayco's 19th anniversary with the company, May 2019, after his untimely passing, this plaque was presented to the family. When a person passes away, many companies just simply replace the employee. They do not honor the past employee and present a plaque to the family . . . Rayco's company wanted us to know exactly what he meant to them . . .

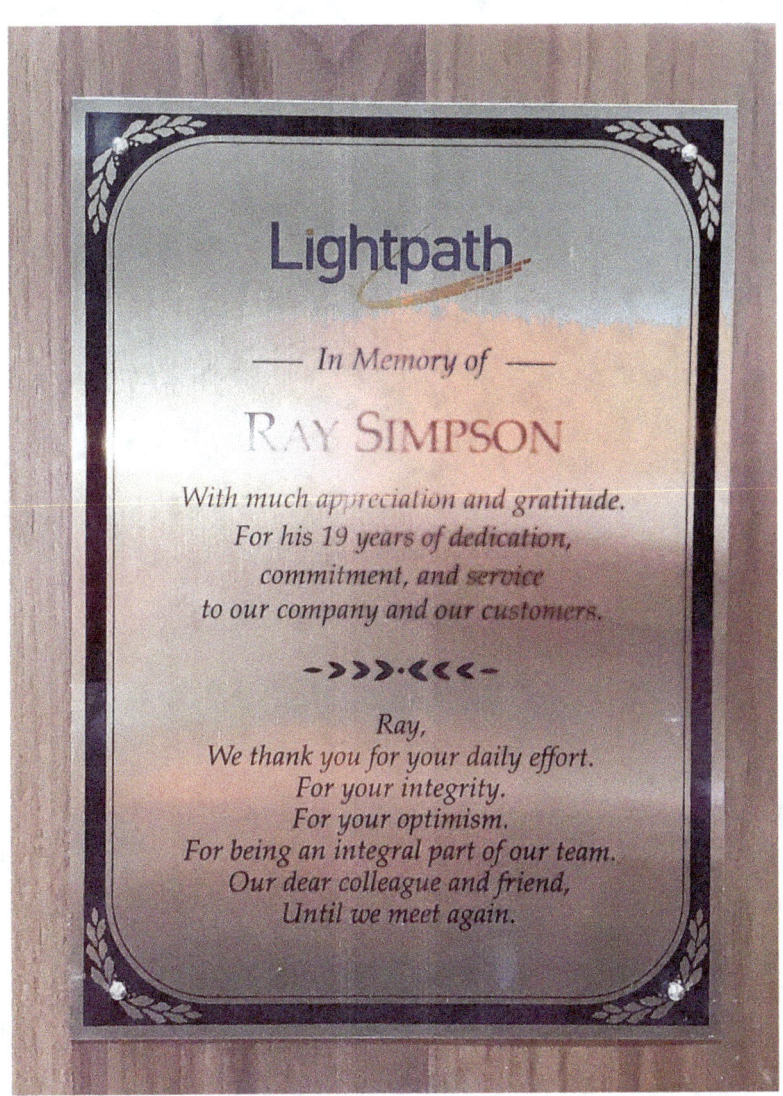

RAYCO'S FINAL HONORARY PLAQUE

13

Growing Pains

*A*nother example of my Rayco was seen earlier in our marriage. I wanted to get an in-ground pool for our children. I had interviewed several pool companies. All of the prices were way out of our budget. Finally, I interviewed my last pool company. I would always interview at least 4 companies for each project. Rayco was at work. I was in the midst of negotiating the price. The negotiated price would include Rayco digging the actual hole for the pool. Rayco walked in from work during the final stages of the negotiation. The pool guy said hello to Rayco. He then said, "So, I hope you are ready to dig the hole for your new pool." Rayco looked at me, confused . . . I looked at him and said, "Rayco, may I explain later?" He responded, "I'm not sure that I am looking forward to hearing this." I asked the pool guy to leave and told him that he would have to come back tomorrow. I needed to speak to my Rayco to make sure he was good with this plan . . . The next day, we signed the contract. We had to rent a backhoe for the weekend and all of the necessary tools to dig a large hole. Early Saturday morning, it began to rain. Actually, it started to thunderstorm. Rayco, nonetheless, still dug the hole. However, every time I would open the window or door to yell out to him and ask if he wanted any water, a sandwich, or any help from me, he would yell back, "Close the window/door and leave me alone!" I left him alone. Rayco dug the hole, all the while falling in the puddles due to the rain. This is another reason why Rayco started saying, "It's raining Ray." This statement exemplified Rayco being proud of himself and how he would conquer defeat . . . We now have a beautiful kidney shaped pool!

THE EARLY POOL

Many years later, our four adult children presented Rayco with an honorary Doctorate degree plaque. It was signed by all four of our adult children. This is so fitting of the man he was. It is also very fitting of the wonderful children we have raised. They were grateful for all the sacrifices their father made to provide for them. When the first two were born, Rayco told them, "Don't call me dad, call me Ray" However, he was always there for ALL of his children. I want to reiterate Ray Anthony Simpson, Sr., did not finish college, he had a GED. However, Ray Anthony Simpson Sr. *did* have a PhD for his drive, dedication and determination that his family would live well . . . Many times he would also say to the children, "If it weren't for your mom, I might have ended up in jail or killed." He said this because we were both raised in poor single parent households. Life was very hard for both of us. We witnessed a lot of things young people should not have had to witness. Nonetheless, he was the most dedicated husband, father and employee you could ever meet.

In a previous chapter, I told of all of his "15 jobs," a familiar term of people from Jamaican ancestry. On top of this, he was a coach for our two sons for many years. Several of the young men that my husband coached when they were youths, made their way to Rayco's final services. Many drove, took a plane and did whatever they had to do to make sure they were there to show respect for a man they considered a mentor or a second father. It warmed my heart to see all of our "extended family of children" at his services. Our children and our determination to remain together were the most important thing to us. It was also important to us that our children would not suffer in life as we did. Our children saw this. They are proud of us and we are so very proud of them!

I remember Rayco and me driving up to college with each one of our children. Each one going to remarkable private and Ivy League universities. Rayco and I never had the privilege of getting driven to college by our parents. We were proud of all four of them. However, we always had mixed emotions. It was stressful for us. We always seemed to get into some sort of argument. I remember when we were taking BookyBoy up to Cornell University, Rayco got out of the car. I was upset. Bookyboy says, "Mom, I know you are upset. You and dad are very intelligent people, though. You both didn't have a degree when you met and you managed to accomplish so much for us. Dad is the smartest man *ever*. He picked you, mom."

On the way back home, I remember playing Lisa Stanfield's "Been Around the World and I Can't Find My Baby" . . . When I arrived back home from Cornell University, **"my baby"** was there waiting for me to come back home…

· · ·

As previously mentioned throughout the book, Rayco was a warrior . . . He had seen his father and Mr. Arrington drive very nice cars. He never wanted to spend too much on an everyday car for work. Rayco drove a company car. However, like any man, he had to have a toy!!! Bookyboy tells the story of how he and his father decided to go for a ride in his new baby blue luxury car. At this time he had the car for maybe a little over a year, but it was still fairly new. It was always a dream of Rayco's to get this particular luxury car because his dad, the children's grandfather, also had one. Bookyboy said it was a somewhat warm night around 8:00pm. He had recently arrived on Long Island from California, where he currently resided. His dad wanted him to experience driving the car. He remembers his dad wearing a baby blue jogging suit and hat to match. But, of course! He says this was his father's "go to" suit when he drove this particular car. They drove the entire Long Island Expressway with no destination or no place to be. It was the first time our Bookyboy had ever driven the car and he was excited to test it out. He explains how he and his father talked about a bunch of stuff. His father discussed his upbringing and how *his father* also had this particular luxury car. It became a goal of Rayco's to have one, as well. Bookyboy explained he would always remember this day. He told me, "It was one of those stories you visualize as it's being told to you. The story, the way my dad told it, had such a nostalgic feeling to it. It was such a simple little car ride but it really meant a lot to me and it's something I will never forget for the rest of my life. Maybe someday I'll have the same luxury car, too. I'll drive it with my son and tell him about my dad, his grandfather. I will tell him my story, just like my dad told me . . . "

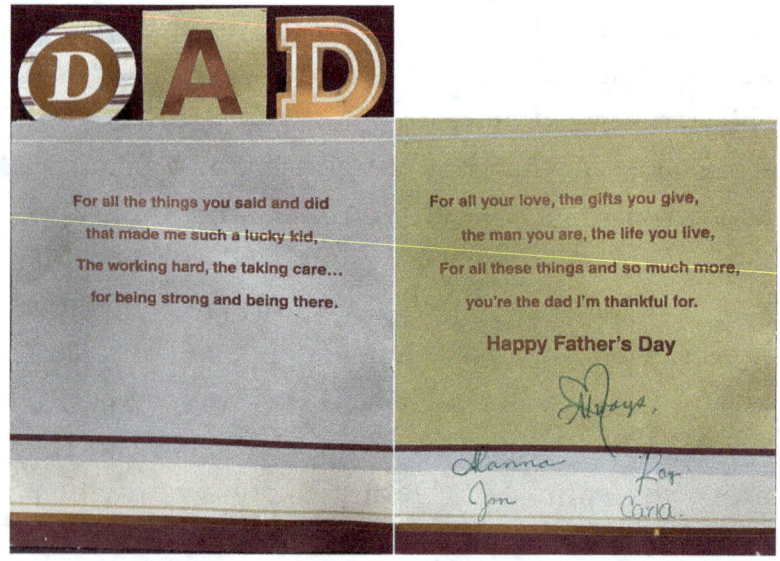

CARD FROM ALL FOUR CHILDREN

They appreciated their father . . . He may not have had a formal Associate's and/or Baccalaureate degree, however, Rayco's drive and love for his family made him persevere. They were proud of the man he was . . . Looking back, God definitely blessed us!

RAYCO'S HONORARY DEGREE

I have always been, and probably will always be, conscious of my weight. So after the delivery of LaniBani, Rayco decided to gift me with a lifetime membership to Bally's. What a lovely gift! I would go regularly. However, LA Fitness bought out Ballys some 20 years after I became a member. Now this is where it gets interesting . . .

LA Fitness called Rayco to convert his membership into a lifetime membership with them. This would cost him minimal dollars per year. I waited for my call. It didn't come. I called LA Fitness to speak to a manager. I even called the central office. They offered me all kinds of memberships. They didn't offer a lifetime membership. I later found out that Rayco had joined Bally's much earlier, which entitled him to a special promotion when LA Fitness bought out Bally's. He found it quite funny watching my persistence in this matter.

Approximately 5 years ago, I scheduled a school trip with my AASO, (African American Student Organization). One of my bff's at the job (I have two) always accompanied me on these trips. On the day of the trip, one of the parents stated they wouldn't be able to go. My colleague, bff, started asking the students if there was a parent who could make a last minute trip. We were going to Washington, to the White House. Yes, we had to get security clearance. I thought it might be easier to get my Rayco to go. I knew that he was home. I called him. The conversation went like this: "Hi, Rayco!" He replied, "What's up?" I asked him about accompanying me and explained the circumstances. He repliesd "Nit, do you really want me to go on a bus with over 40 students to Washington?" I said, "Yes" He said, "I don't even *like* kids!" I said, "You love kids, you have four!" He replied, "Yes, they are mine. They know my rules." He hung up the phone. Needless to say, a little while later, my bff went outside to check if the bus had arrived. Rayco was sitting on the benches in front of the school building. He was completely packed, ready to go, ready to accompany me as a chaperone. At the same time, another parent showed up. I asked him if he still wanted to go. He simply wanted to make sure that I was good. He left. As he walked away, his hands were in the air, like he just won a prize fight!

14

Rayco's 50th Birthday

Rayco had never had a big birthday celebration. My girlfriend of several years had hosted my first birthday party, as previously mentioned, when I was 21. Rayco had given me a 30th, 40th, and later a 50th and 60th. Rayco didn't like to be the center of attraction, however, it was only fitting that he be given a party. He had given me four children, we had a lovely family and life was good. I had never given a birthday party before. It was important to me that everything was perfect. I had the party at the "Compound," as Rayco had recently started calling our home. We had over 100 people. RayJ, our oldest son, was the DJ . . . taking a chapter from his father. We had food, dancing and all had a great time. It was so important that Mr. and Mrs. Arrington, who were previously mentioned, were among the invited guests.

Senator Carl Andrews, a close friend of Rayco's during his youth, was also invited. He was unable to attend; however, his present for Rayco was a plaque which he sent with another close friend of Rayco. We both were surprised. Rayco was humbled. Rayco was presented with a Proclamation honoring him as an esteemed husband and father on his 50th birthday!

RAYCO'S 50TH PROCLAMATION

It would be the last big party for Rayco that my mom would be attending . . .

Sometime after Rayco's 50th celebration, he was on his way to work. He stopped over to the side of the road and called me. He was complaining of chest pains. I asked him where he was going. He responded that he was on his way to his hospital assignment at LI Jewish Hospital. Rayco was the lead technician at the time for all of the surrounding hospitals. I quickly responded, "Rayco, go the hospital and check into emergency as a patient, rather than an employee." He did. I waited to hear from him or the hospital. I remember that I went out and did several errands to keep myself busy. Finally, I got a call from the hospital telling me that Rayco was stabilized and will be okay. They had to put a stint in his aorta. This call was so very comforting.

I went to visit Rayco with my mom. I remember saying to him that he truly scared me today. He said, "I made my peace with God, I am ready to go if that what God wants."

This is the first time that I even thought of Rayco and me being apart. It was the first time that I even thought of the concept of death . . . God blessed us with approximately 15 more years . . .

15

25th Anniversary

On another occasion, I believe it was our twenty-fifth wedding anniversary, we were in Manhattan stayin at a nice hotel. However, we walked to and from all the events to save money on taxi costs. Suddenly, a black SUV pulled up and the doors open. A famous songwriter, Pharrell, jumped out of the SUV with a lady. At first I didn't notice. Rayco motioned to me. I pulled my camera out of my bag and immediately ask Rayco to take a pic of Pharrell and me. He did. Pharrell thought we were quite cute when I told him how long we were married. He wished us well.

We had a lot of fun in New York City. We were like two young teens, running around and enjoying each other. Our place to stay was the Embassy Suites in lower Manhattan. We loved the all-inclusive breakfast and the balcony suites. By the way, we also visited "Good Morning America!"

RAYCO AND I OUTSIDE "GOOD MORNING AMERICA" STUDIOS

Rayco and I were privy to go to one of the game

shows with our youngest son and his beautiful girlfriend when we visited in California. We went on "Let's Make a Deal." The funny thing about this is that we all had to dress up. Rayco dressed up as a basketball player. I was a cheerleader. BookyBoy was a pirate and his girlfriend was a princess. She was adorable and he was so handsome. I remember there being so many rules. I remember the wait to get into the main room where the taping was done was very long. People were dressed in so many interesting costumes. Some people bought their costumes there. They had many costumes for purchase if you forgot.

About halfway through taping, they asked "Who is ready to make the next deal?" My son's girlfriend was sitting in between the two of us. We both pointed to her hoping she would be called as the next contestant. It was not the first time one of my sons and I had pointed to his girl to be selected for something. On one of our cruises, RayJ and I pointed to his then girlfriend, now beautiful wife, to be selected to go on the stage. I remember the look she gave RayJ. At the end, I believe she enjoyed the experience!

This time, to my surprise, the MC called *me* down! I

was asked to show a cheer. The MC of the show was amazed at my age and that I could still cheer. I heard Rayco cheering me on from the audience. After a few tries at winning, I ended up with a consolation prize. We all had a ball!

16

30th Anniversary

*R*ayco and I celebrated thirty years of marriage at the Villas Sol Costa Rica. We had a personal travel coordinator named Lilly. Interestingly, my close aunt's name was Lillian. I remember her being very attentive. I also remember Costa Rica had black sand beaches. Rayco and I commented that it looked so weird to us. We stayed there for a few days and then we went to the Villa Del Mar Cancun. We stayed at this resort also for a few days. Rayco and I were on the beach every day and we danced every night. We had a wonderful time. It was our first vacation without our children. At first, we didn't know how to act. We were always looking for something to do. We did figure it out though. It was a very romantic trip. Rayco would keep saying, "If we were younger and had this much time alone, we would have had ten kids by now" . . . Rayco and I made a point to take tours. We went ziplining as well . . .

In the summer of 2011, when Rayco and I visited Mexico, it was our very first ziplining experience. I remember insisting that we experience it. Every day I would ask, "Are we going on the zipline tour today?" Finally, Rayco said, "Okay, be careful what you are asking for." When we arrived, there was a line to go on the zipline. Rayco went on the zipline before me. When it was my turn to actually zipline, I cried like a baby. One of the natives harnessed himself to me so that I could get across. When we got across to the other side, I couldn't wait to be released. Rayco said, "You were so insistent on ziplining. Yet again, a big chicken!" We walked back to the bus. I don't think that he was very happy with me that afternoon. I really didn't want to experience ziplining again. Rayco didn't care either way. By the way, we did have fun on the Segway.

RAYCO AND I ON SEGWAYS

BACK FROM MEXICO . . . WE ARE SO HAPPY!

17

My Mom

My mom has been mentioned several times in my memoirs. She was a hard working woman. When I was to be admitted to high school, I was to attend PS117 in Brooklyn. I remember walking on the first day to school with my mom. As we got closer to the school, I stopped, along with everyone else. A young girl who had just been raped was pushed off the roof. My mom abruptly turned around with me and said, "You will not be attending this school." My mom then enrolled me into a parochial school in Maspeth, Queens entitled Martin Luther High School. My mom had to scrub the floors at Junior's Restaurant during the day and work as a nurse's aide at night in order to pay the tuition.

When we moved to Long Island, my mom retired as a nurse's aide. She then became a foster mom. She wanted to help young adults suffering with mental illnesses. At the time Willowbrook Developmental Center was getting bad reports on the way they treated their patients. My mom decided to take in some clients from Willowbrook. My mom is the reason that I became a Special Education teacher.

My mom truly helped us to be successful in many

ways. If Rayco and I had a disagreement, my mom would be the one to say, "Nita, one thing is for sure; he is the hardest worker I have ever seen and he truly LOVES You!" When we were moving out to our "dream home," Rayco, as I mentioned earlier, asked my mom to move in with us. He would help her with the maintenance in her area and she helped us in every area. My mom was first diagnosed with a terminal illness, Stage 1, when I was five. She beat it!

It came back with a vengeance in 2005, shortly after my mom's friend, Ben, passed.

I remember taking her to the hospital after she suffered a stroke. Rayco had been home with her. I had left to go to a routine doctor's appointment. He called me suddenly. I rushed home to find the ambulance in my driveway. When we got to the first hospital, the emergency room doctors, after checking my mom in, left her alone for a period of time. I started to complain. I then called our doctor at the time. We shared doctors because my mom never drove a car. I drove her everywhere she went. I was truly the taxi while raising our children. Everyone, except Rayco, was driven around by me . . . So it just made sense that we shared doctors. Our doctor sent an ambulance to get my mom and take her to the hospital that he was affiliated with.

After a complete physical, the doctor's found that the illness had come back. At this time, I had just started my full-time career as a special education teacher, after only working part-time. Rayco was cooking dinner many nights. Sometimes I did when he worked overtime. The doctors at the second hospital told me that my mom may not last the weekend. I lost it. I screamed. I called Rayco. I remember saying to the doctor, "Who died and made you God?" I also remember this is when I began researching organic foods and nutrition in general.

They released my mom from the hospital the first time. Over a period of approximately 3 years, she had subsequent visits to the hospital for chemotherapy treatment. I was taking her to a naturopathic doctor in New York City, as well. Her last visit to the hospital was in June of 2008. I came to pick her up from the hospital so that she wouldn't miss her youngest grandson's high school graduation. I remember the doctor saying, "You don't realize how sick your mom is." Maybe, I didn't; but

I knew that she would want to see Bookyboy graduate.

My youngest son's Godmother, Rayco, and I basically carried my mom into the auditorium for the graduation. Somewhere during this month, I believe while she was still in the hospital, before I took her out for the graduation, my mom made a point to thank me for being a great daughter. I remember her calling me one day after I had just taught a class. I picked up all of hers and the doctor's calls because every call would be important. She said, "The one thing I did perfectly in this life was to have *you*!" To this day, I linger on that phone call. She was trying to say "goodbye." I also linger on the fact that my mom lasted approximately 3 years after the original diagnosis when they told me that she would not possibly last the weekend. She made the high school graduation for all four of her grandchildren. She also made it to the college graduation of her first granddaughter, Carlzbear!

After BookyBoy's high school graduation, my mom's illness went on a steady decline. The first week of August, our LaniBani, was leaving to go back to college to begin her final year. She said to my mom, "I will come back for your birthday, Grandma." That would be August 28th. My mom said that she wouldn't see her. I remember also being so excited about the Presidential elections. I told my mom that I would carry her in November to the polls. She said, "No, you won't!" The last week of my mom's life, I called an old friend that I hadn't seen in years. Her mom and my mom had become great friends. I left a message on her machine asking her to reach out to her mom. I wanted her to ask her mother come and visit my mom. She not only reached out, but actually brought her mom to see mine. We hadn't spoken in over 20 years, but she was there for me when I needed her.

Her mom prayed with my mom. She then said, "Your mom will be okay!" The last night of my mom's life, it was thundering and pouring heavy rain. I asked my mom if she wanted me to lay with her. She said no. Rayco put on a Ray Charles CD and played it all night for my mom. Ray Charles was one of my mom's favorite artists. Rayco and RayJ also assisted me with taking her to and from the bathroom and checking on her. Every time we heard thunder, I would run upstairs. I whispered in my mom's ear, "Please don't leave me tonight." She didn't . . .

• • •

The next morning, I checked on my mom. She was sitting up on the bed. Her voice, though, was barely audible. I remember saying that I was going to call the ambulance. Mom kept saying "No." She wanted to stay home. Our oldest daughter, who then resided in Manhattan, had called me the night before to say I should call the ambulance just to check her out. I never did because mom kept saying "No." In hindsight, I probably should have taken her earlier on when she was okay to go, but I really was going through an emotional attack. I really didn't know what to do. Rayco was right by my side through this whole horrible situation.

I want to mention that the previous year was my 50th birthday. Rayco gave me a huge party on August 28th. The party was given on my mom's actual birthday. He had a cake for my mom and sang "Happy Birthday" to her, as well. It was her 77th birthday. At that well-attended party, my mom and I had our last dance.

MOM AND ME

After checking on my mom, I went for a jog. I asked the nurse I had hired to try to get her to eat. I came back from the jog and the nurse met me at the door and said that my mom wasn't eating. I ran upstairs to help. Rayco had left for work. I remember talking to my mom and saying I will help her to sit in her chair so that she could drink some water and eat. She said, "Maybe later." I said, "Mom, you have to try and drink water and/or eat. Also, we want to change your sheets." I held my mom up. After a minute, she collapsed. The nurse called 911. I was with my mom as she took her last breath, while looking at me. I called Rayco. I was numb until he got there. I then collapsed into his arms. My mom took her last breath on Tuesday,

August 12, 2008. She passed on LaniBani's birthday. My mom somehow knew that she would not see LaniBani on August 28th nor would she be voting in November.

Some months prior to my mom's passing, I was asked to chaperone the spring musical at my new job. I brought my mom with me. I introduced her to all of the current administrators while there. The principal at the time said, "It's not official, but I think we will be asking your daughter to return next year." My mom said, "You had better! She is the best and she loves children!" I remember feeling very nervous because as the administrator said, it wasn't official, and my mom was giving her a directive. I share this because at my mom's funeral services, this particular administrator came and said to my mom at her 'resting bed', "I told you we were going to keep her."

OUR LAST DANCE TOGETHER

Now, after my mom passed, I was having a truly difficult time. It seemed that Rayco and I were estranged. Our children, now young adults, also felt it. I started attending church every Sunday. I remember one Sunday going to the altar for prayer. I asked God to please bless me with my husband attending church with me. He would always work on Sundays for overtime. Some weeks later, I got up for church. Rayco looked over at me and asked, "What time are you going to church?" He attended church with me. I was so very elated . . . God is good!

This was a very difficult time for Rayco, me, and also our young adult children. For approximately 3 years, I couldn't see past the pain of losing my mom. Rayco was attending church with me. The first year after my mom's passing, I mentioned to Ray that I would want to celebrate my mom's first year with God by getting rebaptized in our church. I went to all of the classes beforehand. I was to get rebaptized in August 2009, right around the time of my mother's birthday. The morning of that day, we woke up to a huge hurricane. It was called *Hurricane Irene.* Irene was my mother's middle name. It was a true hurricane. All of the churches, school, stores, gas stations—in other words, everything—was shut down. I could not believe it. I couldn't understand it. God was telling me this was NOT the time!

18

Remy/Vacation

My mom's passing was a horrible blow for me as well as Rayco and our four, now close to adult, children. She passed just before my 51st birthday. Rayco was trying to help me cope. He loves dogs and always had one or two or three . . . He kept saying to me, "I am going to get you a dog to take care of. The dog will also take care of you. It will keep you busy and help you to cope." He waited until all of the children were home. Late June, we all traveled East and Rayco purchased a female Rottweiller. She was the smallest of the puppies; however, she was fiesty. She had to fight to get to her food because all of the other puppies in the litter were much bigger. Rayco wanted her! He named her Remy, aka "Remy Martin." We all got a kick out of that name. Like I said, he purchased Remy for me to take care of. However, Rayco always took care of Remy.

About five years later, Rayco decided that Remy needed a playmate. He was also considering possibly breeding Remy. So he said he would want a male Rottweiler. I remember going to the kennel with him. We stayed there for a while. Rayco was watching one of the puppies who had a white mark on her fur. He asked the breeder what happened to her??? The breeder explained the mark came after a rock fell on her and her fur never healed properly. Rayco watched this puppy for over an hour. He decided that he wanted her. I said, "I thought you wanted a male?" Rayco said, "No, we will take her. We will name her Roxy. Rayco always fell in love with the underdog. LaniBani said Roxy could reside in her section of the house. She also said that she would assist Rayco in caring for her. Rayco always took care of Roxy, as well!

Now we have two dogs. Eventually, all of our adult children moved away, accept for Carlzbear, who came home and ended up helping her two parents. Nonetheless, Rayco took care of both dogs now. Our routine in the morning before work became—namely, wake up, brush teeth, Rayco fed the dogs, we would meet in the gym to work out. We then showered together and went to our respective walk-in closets to dress for work. I loved our mornings together. However, I did notice Rayco getting tired of the routine. Many mornings he would say, "I am tired." I offered to help with the dogs on several occasions. He denied help!

Rayco also suggested a family cruise in the summer of 2009. We traveled from August 13th through the 20th with all four young adult children. Rayco suggested and initiated this cruise to help with healing for all of the children and myself after the loss of my mom. We flew to Miami and boarded the Norwegian Sky at the Port of Miami to Nassau, Bahamas. This trip was the first trip where Rayco and I had a balcony room. I loved it! He went out of his way to make this trip a success . . . Our four adult children had an amazing time as well. Jon is the youngest; however, his older siblings helped him to mature on that cruise! They stayed up late at night and snuck into parties with Jon! (Lol) We then visited Sea World, Orlando Florida. We stopped off to visit Rayco's sister and his mom. We had a great time. Carlzbear did an itinerary album with an album cover of "The Simpsons." She handed a copy to everyone just before we started on the trip. Carlz added her expertise to the trip!! This happened a year after my mom's passing and Rayco did a great job of giving me a brief diversion from the pain of becoming an orphan!

THE SIMPSONS!

THE SIMPSONS!

Every time we traveled, we had my close friend or a young man who is like a son to house sit. Remy did not see anyone else for training, washing, etc. Rayco did everything. The only time the dogs saw anyone else was when we had someone to house sit. Remy, in particular, became very attached to Rayco.

If any one of our adult children wanted to pay for a groomer or vet to come to the house for our two dogs, Roxy would oblige. Remy would not!

ROXY AND REMY...

Exactly five months and four days after Rayco made his transition to GOD, Remy passed away . . . She was truly Rayco's dog.

LAST PIC OF REMY

Roxy, however, is now my dog. She is by my side and literally sleeps outside of my bedroom at night. We have our own "new" routine in the morning . . . She growls if she feels someone is not talking to me in the correct tone. I have never taken care of a dog. It is very *easy* though, because Rayco has already trained her . . . I love my Roxy!

Roxy . . . SHE IS HUGE

19

Forging Ahead

My mom was born in August and made her transition to God in the same calendar month.

After the loss of my mom, Rayco made it a point to keep me busy. We took salsa lessons. He took me to see a Broadway play regularly. I would attend church every Sunday to help me get through the grieving. I felt so blessed and elated that Rayco had started going to church with me. Approximately 2 years after my mom passed away, Rayco's mom passed away. This was the second time I had seen Rayco go off the deep end! When his father passed, even though he was not raised by his father, he took it hard . . . The funeral services were in Florida. Rayco, being the warrior that he was, said he wanted to go alone. Nonetheless, with the help of LaniBani, who booked a flight for me to go to Florida to attend the funeral, I went as well. At first he wasn't receptive. At the end, he thanked me for being there and having his back, despite his pushing me away. Marriage, in and of itself, is difficult. In addition to that fact, Rayco and I both came from damaged, abusive and poor childhoods. Both of us had trust issues . . . During all of our challenges, It was definitely God that kept us strong and got us through.

. . .

Our youngest daughter, LaniBani, came home to live with us after she graduated from college. She was very helpful in trying to get me through the grief as well as Rayco after my mom and even his mom's passing. I truly needed her and she was there for me. She and Rayco were very close; when he couldn't be there, he knew LaniBani would definitely be there. She will always be our baby girl!

Our oldest daughter, Carlzbear, also, was extremely worried about me when my mom passed. She knew that my mom and I were more like sisters. Later in life, Rayco, and RayJ began to call Carlzbear and me "Oprah and Gail." We became and are to this day, extremely close . . . more like sisters.

A few years after my mom made her transition, Carlzbear, announced that she was having her first child. She was due in October, October 12th to be exact, one day after Rayco's birthday.

Our first granddaughter was to be born in the same month and the same week as our calendar day. I remember when Carlz went into labor. It was on the evening of former President Obama's first presidential debate before his 2nd Presidential term. It was more importantly on the evening of Rayco's birthday. She came to us and said that she was feeling a slight discomfort. We knew this was the beginning of labor. We walked with her all night. The next day, LaniBani flew in from Florida where she was attending Law School. Late that evening our first granddaughter, our gorgeous Ms. 'Ava My Neighbor,' was born!

AVA MY NEIGHBOR

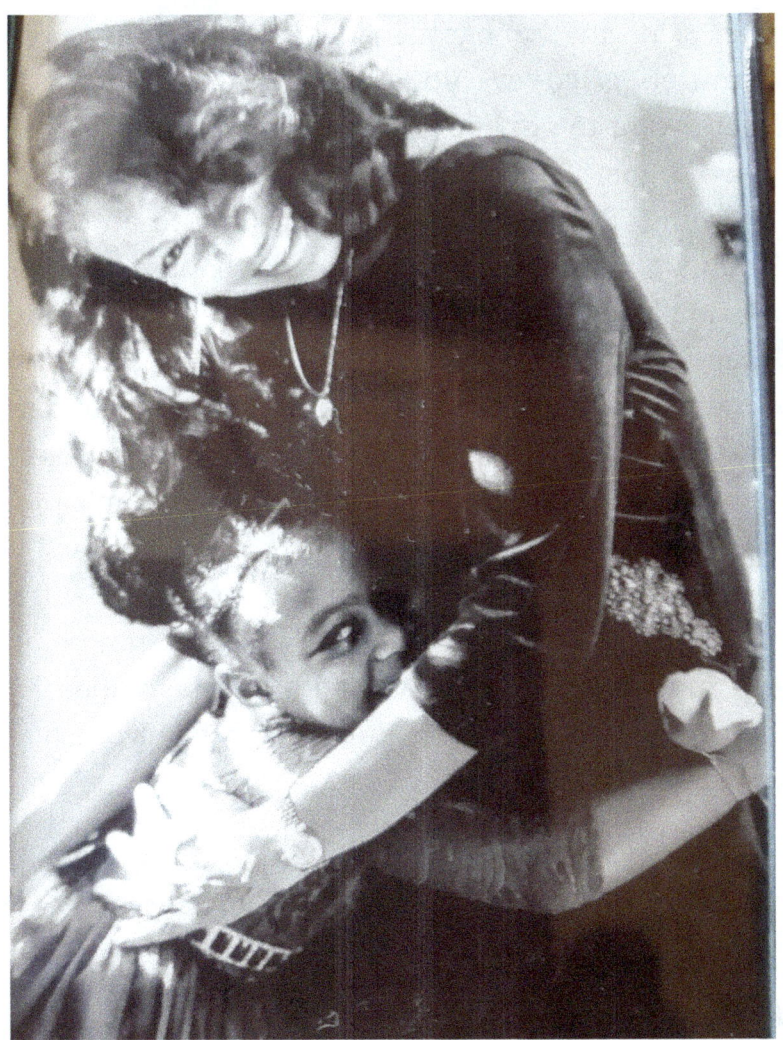

AVA AND ME

In the summer of 2018, I said to Rayco, "I want to try again to get baptized." I went on to say that I wanted him to be baptized with me. His manager, Mike, later mentioned that Rayco had told everyone at work I was telling him that he must be baptized.

We went to the baptismal classes together. The minister asked everyone to tell him what made them want to get baptized, Rayco said, "My wife," On August 26th, 2018, we were baptized. That morning, Rayco sent out a group text to all of his friends with a photo of him in the baptismal robe, posing as a "man of God." After the service, we and many of our invited guests, went to Pinelawn where I acknowledged my mom's ten year anniversary with God. I spoke. Rayco stood in the background. I remember him pointing to my mom's plot and saying he will be right next to "mom." I remember looking at him but ignoring the statement. I couldn't even think of my Rayco not being by my side. We went on with the festivities by returning to our "manor" and eating. Everyone had a blessed time . . .

**RAYCO IN ROBE JUST BEFORE HIS BAPTISM
AUGUST 2018**

Literally, five months before Rayco and I got baptized, RayJ and our first daughter-in-law came to visit. They came to show us pictures of their wedding which took place the prior July. We went through the pictures and RayJ gave us our own copy of his wedding album. We got to the last picture and there was a picture of a fetus . . . Rayco and I were elated! They told us that we were about to have our 2nd granddaughter.

The next month after Rayco and my baptisms, September, we celebrated the birth of RayJ's first-born daughter.

My beautiful daughter-in-law, on the day of Rayco's passing, revealed to me that Rayco was the one who gave his blessing on our 2nd granddaughter's middle name. I was very happy to know that. You see my granddaughter's middle name is the same as my daughter-in-law's grandmother. Rayco's suggestion and blessing that the middle name be one of his daughter-in-law's grandmother just again represents the humility and love for family he had. By the way, our 2nd grand daughter is simply BEAUTIFUL!

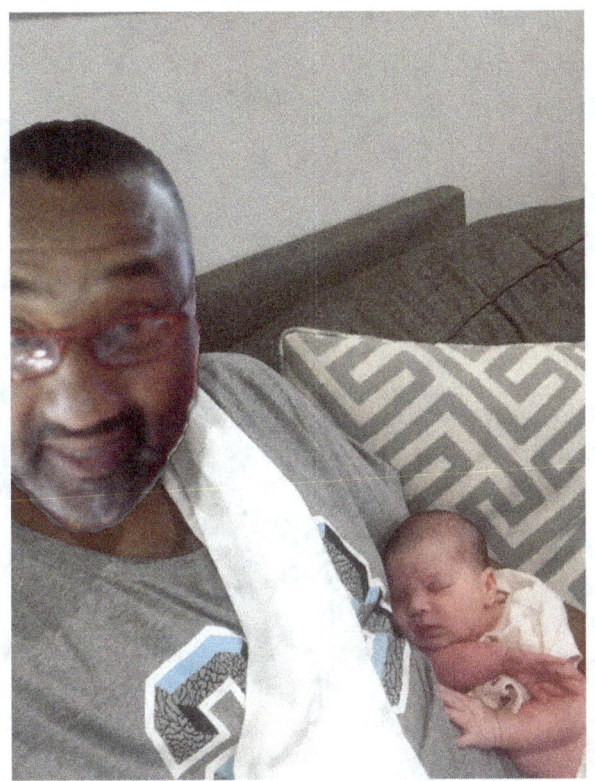

RAYCO'S ONLY PIC WITH KINGSLEY

KINGSLEY IS TIRED...

HOWEVER, SHE IS OUR BEAUTIFUL 2ND GRANDDAUGHTER

KINGSLEY, AVA, RAYCO AND ME

When our oldest son RayJ was about to be 13 years old, we wanted to have a special "coming out" ceremony to represent him leaving childhood and becoming a man. Rayco and I sat down with RayJ and asked him what he wanted. RayJ, without hesitation, told Rayco and me that he wanted to be closer to God. We were members of St. Thomas More Roman Catholic Church at the time. We put everything in order for RayJ to make his Rites of Passage . . . This is how he celebrated his 13th birthday!

Rayco and I, as I have stated many times

throughout this book, created our own family traditions, as we didn't have any. Again, we were raised by single parents with not much of a history given to us, except the stories told to each of us by our moms. This is one of the main reasons I wrote this book. Many times, if Rayco was upset with our son, RayJ, he might say to him, "I can't believe we gave you my name." This has resonated with our son, and I must say he really stepped up to the plate and has become a wonderful young man. It is a lot of pressure on a family, parents and children, when we are trying to make our own way, our own traditions, right and/or wrong, etc. I am mentioning this because RayJ has become his father, for the most part. He is a determined young man. He works around the clock to take care of his family . . . He also recently stated to me that he loves his name . . . I love the fact that he is continuing his father's namesake..More importantly, I know that Rayco loves it as well….This is why he gave our first son his name!!!

SO PROUD OF OUR HANDSOME SON!!!

20

Rayco's 60th Birthday

We went on a family cruise with Carnival in 2009. I wanted to mention that on the boat I had signed up to sing "The Closer I Get To You" by Roberta Flack. It was the same song that was sung at our wedding service. I practiced the song with a young man who was a professional singer. However, when I saw the huge crowd that evening, I froze. Our two daughters, Carlzbear and LaniBani came to my aid immediately and began to do lyrical dancing behind me while I was singing. They did this in order to distract the crowd while I was freezing up . . .

It is for this reason that for Rayco's 60th, I knew that I had to take singing lessons. I wanted to sing Natalie Cole's "Inseparable." You see, I wanted Rayco and all of our invited guests to know that this is how I felt about my Rayco. We are inseparable, we are soulmates, connected spirits, no matter what universe he or I reside in . . .

Singing lessons began for me in January 2014. I would go once per week. I started singing lessons to make sure I could prepare, and not freeze again, when I see the crowd at Rayco's 60th . . .

RAYCO'S 60TH SPEECH

I also want to mention that it was right around Rayco's 60th birthday that he received a promotion to work inside the office as the Lead Technical Dispatcher. I remember calling him the "head man in charge." He would always correct me. He, however, had mixed feelings. He would say, "Now I can't make as much overtime." I would say, "You are making more money. We are good." I want to mention sometime after his 64th birthday, he started taking more overtime assignments on the weekend. It was in his blood. He just couldn't be in the office five days a week. He then restarted working on weekends as well . . . I do know that everything Rayco did, however, he did for his family!

After my job's end of year party the previous year, I decided on the venue. I selected the Wind Watch Golf & Country Club. It had a beautiful golf course and an amazing view. Looking back, I can't believe I took singing lessons, but I knew that I wanted his party to be perfect in every sense of the word.

At first, we were planning for Rayco's party to be a surprise. However, he kept asking so many questions that after a while, the children and I gave in and told him. It was extremely difficult to keep a secret from Rayco. He kept saying, because Rayco was always so selfless, "I don't need a party." Rayco knew he was the major 'bread winner.' He didn't want us to be put out financially.

Rayco deserved a party, though. I was determined to give him the party he deserved. We called all of his friends from his past and present. They all came. Our son RayJ gave a very emotional speech. He delivered a very emotional speech again for Rayco's final services. I am so very glad that his first emotional speech was at his father's birthday celebration.

Three years later, Rayco planned a 60th birthday party for me. He did this in conjunction with our four children. RayJ and my first daughter-in-law introduced me to the crowd the day of the party. I remember modeling as I walked into the ballroom. I am mentioning this because it was at my party that Rayco gave a very emotional speech, telling how he was inspired by my mom and me and our drive to have a better life. He told the crowd that he bought into this concept because he wanted himself and any future children to have a better life, as well. Rayco told the crowd that day that when he met me and then my mom, he knew right away that he wanted to spend his life with me. He also knew that this meant he would have to include my mom. It is rare when a woman finds a man who will go through life with her and respect and include her mom in their life as well . . . Rayco is/was and will always be my Pearl!

When it was time for me to sing this time, I did not freeze. Rayco's had tears in his eyes and his eyes were fixed on me as I sang to him. At the end of the party, Rayco thanked everyone. This is when I learned of the men who helped to rear him during his early years. Rayco had never forgotten from where he came . . .

Everyone had a wonderful time!

THIS IS US!!!

21

35th and 37th Anniversaries

Our four children, specifically Carlzbear, organized and orchestrated Rayco's and my 35th wedding anniversary. I remember being told that we should have a 40th anniversary, rather than a 35th . . . However, Carlzbear was determined that we would celebrate a 35th.

We had two chefs who cooked a special meal for Rayco and me. I remember my daughter-in-law buying white flowers for the table. Carlzbear had essentially hired a student band from the school where I taught I remember speaking to one of the students who didn't believe that Rayco and I could be celebrating 35 years of marriage, simply due to our youthful appearance. RayJ was our DJ, as he knew all of the music that would be important for Rayco and me to hear.

The photographer, Noel, was hired by Carlzbear to recreate all of the photos from Rayco and my wedding album made some 35 years ago.

I remember being so very excited. I remember all of the family and friends that were invited to the Simpson compound, as Rayco would call it. We danced all night. We thanked our children for being born . . . We always did that. You see, kids don't ask to be born. Also, God is the one who blessed us with them...

At the end of the night, Rayco dropped to his knees. He asked me to marry him again. He presented me with another ring. He then asked his friend ShellyB, the best man in our original wedding, "Could you please help me up? I am not as young as I used to be." What a wonderful evening!!!

OUR 35TH FAMILY PIC

I want to mention that in the previous picture, Rayco is wearing a hat. He loved hats. He would also say that I should wear hats more often as I look very good in them. I never really wore hats. However, now I find security in wearing Rayco's hats. They are my *"security blanket."* I know this might sound bizarre, but I have a hat in each car, and pretty much every room. I now wear hats on a regular basis.

. . .

Sometime after our 35th wedding anniversary, I had gotten very sick. I was eventually diagnosed with a rare illness. I was told by the doctor that I was his only "ethnic" patient with this illness. He wanted me to get a transplant and told Rayco that I might not live without one. I was diagnosed on July 7th, the same month and year that our eldest son, RayJ was getting married. He and our beautiful daughter-in-law were married on July 29th. Rayco and I went to the wedding and had a wonderful time. However, shortly after, my illness took a turn for the worse. I was hospitalized the day after my 60th birthday. I am mentioning this because my Rayco who got up practically seven days a week for our entire marriage and didn't complain, now would go to work, and then come to the hospital and stay with me. I was in the ICU. I became determined to get better somehow. All he wanted to do was make sure that I was okay. Looking back, I know that my illness took a toll on my Rayco. He had a weak heart. He said to me, "I will not live without you!" Looking back, he was so very selfless. His unselfish attitude towards life, even with people he didn't know, is something everyone can learn from.

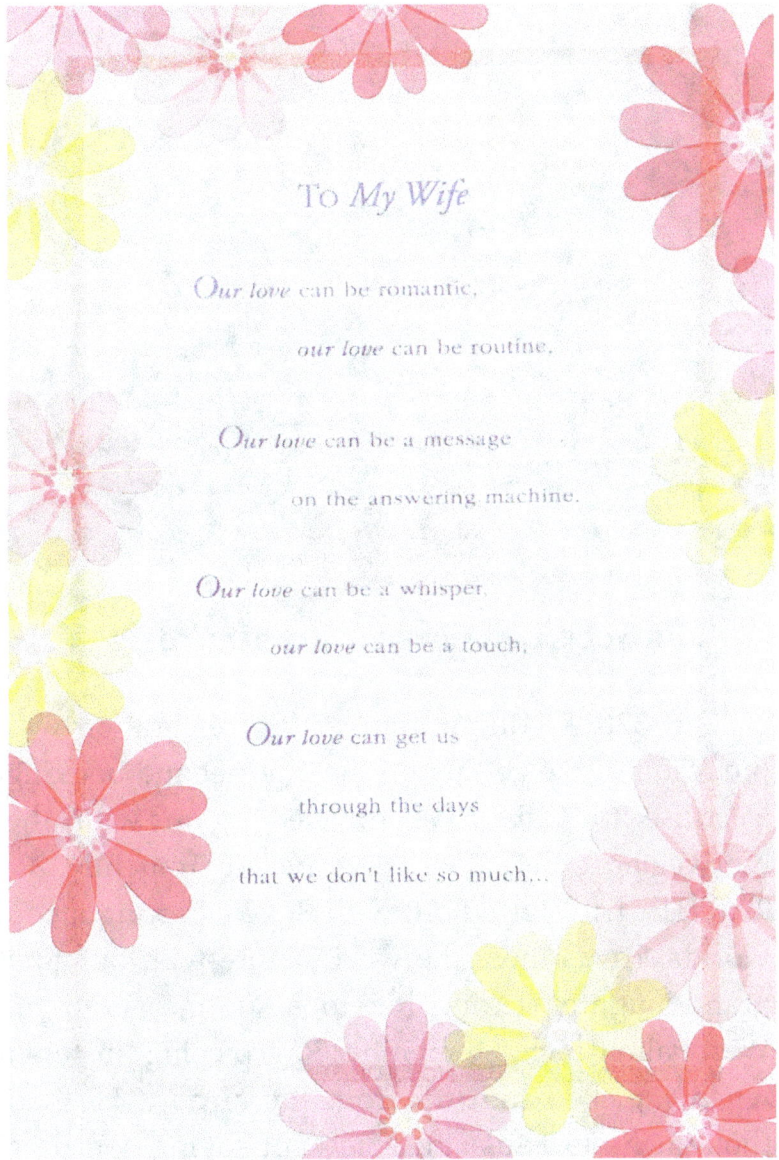

RAYCO'S LAST MOTHER'S DAY CARD TO ME

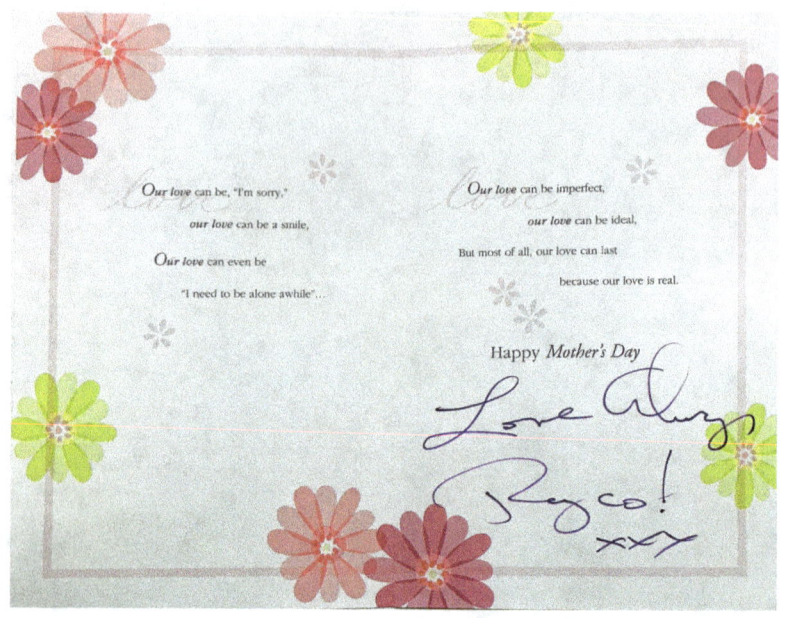

RAYCO'S LAST MOTHER'S DAY CARD TO ME

Our 37th wedding anniversary celebration was the result of me getting on the internet and booking a cruise to Cuba. We traveled again with the Norwegian cruise line. We traveled from July 23-27th. The trip started out with Rayco meeting me in Florida. I was there the week before with our first granddaughter, taking her to a summer camp in West Palm Beach. I remember Rayco being flustered when I picked him up from the airport. He had thought he lost his ring. He kept saying someone stole his ring. He was flustered and couldn't seem to relax. Rayco was a warrior. He wanted everything right. He knew that I booked this trip and it was a big anniversary. Actually, every anniversary was a big anniversary! He didn't talk much before we boarded the cruise ship. After we settled in, I asked him if we could take a walk and look around the boat. We took a walk and there were a lot of shops, etc. I remember going into one of the jewelry stores and looking at rings. I saw a simple male wedding band. I don't even know if it was genuine gold. I decided to purchase it for Rayco. When I presented it to him, he said, "I guess you want everyone to know that I am married to you, right?" I said, "You got that right!" He smiled. I loved my Rayco. It bothered me to see him upset about the rings. I knew that he, like me, would keep thinking about it. I wanted him to enjoy his trip. He relaxed somewhat after he got the ring.

Also, on this trip, Rayco decided that he wanted to purchase art for his now two granddaughters. The art expo started out with an auction. Rayco was involved with every auction. He kept raising his hand with each offer. I had never been to an auction, I don't believe Rayco had either. At one point, the offer went up to over $1,000. Rayco went to raise his hand. I reached over to him without even thinking, almost jumping on him, and put his hand down. Rayco looked over at me and laughed. "There goes my "Nitagal." However, just as I did this, the auction host says, "Okay, the two people who kept their hand up, this artwork will be given to you 'free'". I was shocked. Rayco looked at me and said, "See, ye of little faith." He told this story to everyone who asked him about our cruise. It was the first story he would share.

On the actual day of our anniversary, Rayco asked me to take a walk and let us look around the ship—the same thing that I had said to him on the first day. We went looking at first for coffee. Adjacent to the coffee counter was another jewelry shop. Rayco said, "Let's look in this shop." We were looking around and the next thing I knew he was purchasing me a Swarovski earrings and bracelet set. This wasn't planned. I didn't ask for it. The cruise and being together and having fun together was amazing. This was the icing on the cake.

By the way, sometime after we arrived back home in Long Island, I told Rayco that I was filing a claim for the jewelry that he had said was stolen. I got all of the paperwork together. The day before I was going to send the paperwork in, Rayco came into the tv room and said, "I found the rings!" He was so happy. It just so happened that he had packed them away so carefully, he forgot how carefully he had packed them . . . My Rayco!

. . .

On a side note, the day of Rayco's funeral services, I wore the Swarovski earrings and bracelet. The evening of the services I didn't know what had happened to my bracelet. I had essentially lost it. I was very upset. Several weeks after the burial of my Rayco, I went to the Swarovski store at the mall to purchase another bracelet. That evening, I was on the phone with my LaniBani and she said, "Do you know anyone who lost a bracelet, Mom?" It was my Swarovski bracelet. I was sooo happy. Needless to say, I had my original bracelet fixed. I then, of course, returned the new bracelet that I had bought to replace the original!

22

Ava's First Father/Daughter

*I*n early March, our oldest daughter asked Rayco to attend the first "Father and Daughter" dance courtesy of the Girl Scouts, with our first granddaughter, Ava My Neighbor (Rayco's nickname for her). Rayco was honored. The night of the dance was March 14th, the last Friday of Rayco's life on earth. I remember Rayco taking a nap before the dance so that he would be well rested to attend. The night of the dance, I remember also coming down to the bedroom and saying to Rayco that Ava was about to get dressed. Rayco abruptly got up and began to get dressed. The evening of the dance, I took pictures of our first granddaughter and Rayco. They danced to Ed Sheeran's "Thinking Out Loud.". She was so very pretty and happy! Rayco, as always, was very handsome! Ava will never forget it and neither will I. Now, looking back, I am so very glad that we took video and many pictures as this is something that I plan to show at, hopefully, all of her future events.

It is also important to mention that I met with the publisher of this book on May 3, 2019. We met at Panera Bread. When we sat down to order, the same Ed Sheeran song, "Thinking Out Loud," came on. I believe it was my signal to definitely write my book!

LAST PIC OF AVA AND RAYCO FROM HIS LAST TEXT TO ME

Not long after Rayco's passing, I was babysitting Ava one afternoon. She and I were in the garage. Rayco has several pictures displayed throughout our garage. There are pictures of all of our adult children, our moms and us at various functions. Ava asks, "MaDa, who put up these pictures?" I responded, "Da did, but now he is gone." I put my head down. Ava tapped me on my leg. She responded, "It's okay, MaDa. Now is our time to shine and let Da know how much we appreciated what he did for us." I didn't know what to say. She is still in elementary school . . . She is so smart . . . Out of the mouths of babes . . .

RAYCO AND AVA AT THE MOVIES

AVA, RAY AND ME AT OUR CURRENT CHURCH

23

Our Last Months

In October, 2018, Rayco and I went for his routine visit to the cardiologist. I called my job to say I would be a little late, but I ended up not going to work because the doctor told me they had to keep Rayco for further testing. He was in the hospital overnight. The next day, he called me and said, "I am here and they haven't done anything. I want to go home!" I said, "Rayco, don't they have to check you out?" I spoke to the hospital and doctors later that day. By the way, Rayco also called our oldest daughter and said if mom doesn't pick me up, call me an Uber!" I spoke to the doctor later that evening when I arrived. He proceeded to give me all of the numbers to all of the doctors for the tests my Rayco needs. It was our intention to call them in the summer and get all of his doctor appointments completed. I still have the numbers in my calendar book. The doctor then spoke to Rayco and said, "You need to do these things, somewhat soon, or you could die." I still have written the doctors we were planning to see. I had made some appointments for him immediately. He also went for a 2nd opinion within two weeks of the hospital stay. The 2nd opinion doctor told Rayco his heart was doing better. How ironic! He used medical terms and I advised him that we have a host of doctors we were going to see. However that day, Rayco responded, "I hate to break it to you doctor, but we are all destined to die!"

During November and December, 2018, we attend one of Rayco's extended family's weddings—the husband is now a retired football player. We had a wonderful time and it would be the last time Rayco and I had a chance to do the hustle together. We also had the family over for the holidays. Rayco and all of his sons took a picture before we went for a turkey race. We always have sooo much fun together.

    I had been diagnosed with a rare illness. We celebrated our "Simpson X-mas" in January to accommodate our adult children being able to have their own X-mas with their spouses and children. It was on this day that Rayco told everyone that he is purchasing mom (me) a Christmas present that will help with my illness. I am elated!

RAYCO WITH THE BOYS

RAYCO WITH OUR TWO GIRLS

I finally received the chamber in February. Rayco said we must make an appointment with our attorney to update our wills. I asked him why he was so insistent, we have plenty of time. He responded, "You can't be sure of that." In addition to the everyday responsibilities of being a Special Education teacher, every February I host an annual educational presentation to commemorate Black History month. I advise the African American Student Organization (AASO), at my job. This particular year, I videotaped the entire show. The morning of the show, I mentioned to Rayco that I felt very nervous. The show is a big event for the entire staff, administration and community. Rayco responded, "Just embrace it." At the conclusion of the show, I always commended the students for their great job. I always thanked my fellow colleagues, administration and the parents for their support. I always mentioned my family, as well. This year I made it a point to thank my Rayco, in particular, for his support and love. I also thanked him telling me to "embrace" the anxiety and nervousness. The entire audience clapped for my Rayco. How ironic, that I pointed out my Rayco and thanked him especially. How ironic because this was the last show he would attend . . .

About 3 weeks before Rayco passed, he woke up early and said, "Nit, I have to get to work early because the manager, Mike's, sister has cancer and is in the hospital. She is not expected to make it." He would leave at least a half hour earlier for work to cover for the manager. Rayco was the 2nd man in charge. Later that week Mike's sister passed away. Sometime later after Rayco passed, Mike, the manager, said he never had to worry about the office when Rayco was there. He would call while at the hospital with his sister and Rayco would say, "Why are you calling me, focus on your sister. Don't worry about the office. I got this." The manager said he would never forget Rayco's loyalty.

One morning during the first week of March, we both woke up around 4:30am. I proceeded to say my morning prayers and then work out. I heard Rayco saying "I am so tired." It was unusual for Rayco to keep saying that. You see, he never complained. He rarely took a day off from work. Many weeks he worked 7 days during the week. I learned my work ethic from Rayco. You see, I stayed home for many years to raise our children . . .

I said to him, "Do you want me to do something to help you this morning?" He replied, "I got it Nita-gal. Relax." Also during that week, we woke up one morning and started our usual routine which is working out together in the morning before taking a shower. I worked out on the elliptical. Rayco worked out on the treadmill. He was on the treadmill only approximately 2 minutes when he stopped and walked out of our gym. I finished on the elliptical and walked into our bedroom. Rayco was lying down. I asked, "Are you okay?" He said, "Yes, just waiting for you to take a shower." However, he looked tired . . . Looking back, God was sending me a message . . .

On or about the second week of March, I told Rayco that I was going to Whole Foods and asked him if there was anything he would want. He told me what to pick up and one of the items was bread. I went to Whole Foods and got the items. I always purchased Uda grain-free bread for him. However, I saw that "Angelica" grain-free bread was on sale. I purchased it. When I returned home and unpacked, Rayco made it a point to say that he wanted the bread I always get him. I said this bread was on sale. He said, "I like what I like." I mention this story because on the Friday before his transition, he texted me and said, "Well, when you are right, you are right. I tasted the Angelica bread, and it was good. Thx!" Looking back, this text message was very important for me to see.

. . .

On March 17, at approximately 9:04 am, my Rayco, Pearl, best friend, lover, sex guru, made his transition to GOD. It was Sunday morning, St Patrick's Day. That Friday evening he took his little 'Ava My Neighbor' to her first "Father Daughter Dance." Saturday, I remember that I had offered to buy him a Jamaican fish dinner. He said it would cost too much. But somehow, I had it in my heart to buy it for us nonetheless. Saturday evening, I had to chaperone the Spring musical at my job. It was entitled *Me and My Girl*. During the entire chaperoning night, I couldn't stop thinking of Rayco and how the young actor in the play reminded me of him. I rushed home after the chaperoning assignment. I told Rayco that I was going to cuddle up with him because I couldn't stop thinking of him during the chaperoning. He said, "Okay." In the middle of the night, at approximately 1:00am, Rayco woke me up for us to go to our newly purchased King size adjustable bed. Sunday morning he asked me for a kiss so that he could get to work in Manhattan. He and his team were working on a project in the Google building. I said, "It's St. Patrick's Day!" He said, "I am going to make my Irish exit and get right back home." He said, "Pray for me when you go to church." I would be going to church with our oldest later in the day. However, approximately 2 ½ hours later, I received a call. His co-worker was yelling through the phone and telling me to pick up the phone. I did. He said that Rayco collapsed. I said, "What are you talking about? I just kissed him goodbye. He was fine." He then said that the paramedics were there and they had a slight pulse and told the co-workers, "We got this." I knew they didn't have this!!! I felt it in my gut. I dropped the phone. Our oldest picked it up and continued the call to get the location of where they would be taking her dad. We got on the road. It would be the longest and most horrific car ride that I had ever been on. Approximately 10 minutes from the location, I called there. The receptionist answered and at first said that she would put the nurse on the phone. She came back to the phone and said that she would instead put the "head doctor" on the phone. I knew that my gut was correct. He got on the phone and after explaining what the paramedics did, even though he wasn't there, he said my Rayco had "expired." Carlzbear and I screamed. It is important to note that she was DRIVING. He told us this while she was DRIVING. It didn't occur to him that he could have been responsible for more lives being lost in our family that day. When Carlzbear, our Ava My Neighbor, and I arrive at the location, we, after about 20 minutes, were taken to my Rayco. Before sitting with the doctor, I called the principal's secretary to say that I had lost my hubby. I was practically incoherent. She, nonetheless, 'had my back.' She called all of the necessary people that she knew would need to be called. When we sat down with the head doctor, he was asking questions. I answered some while my body was shaking . . . After a few minutes, I told the doctor that I was not going to answer another question until I could see my husband. I asked to be able to spend some time with him. I then asked if I could stay with him so that our family and immediate friends could come and pay their respects. At first we were told no. It is so very wonderful having a daughter who is an attorney!!! We were with Rayco for about 5 to 6 hours after arriving at the location. Our children, my sister-cousin Vivi, cousin Equasia, (Rayco called her Equalization, that was Rayco's way of saying she is intelligent!), and my two closest friends from work, who I will love for the rest of my life, were all there to say their final goodbyes to my Rayco . . .

Except for Rayco's head, his entire body was warm the entire time that we were there . . . Again, that was my Rayco, my warrior!!!

THIS WAS THE WORST DAY OF MY LIFE!

• • •

I must mention that over 400 people were at his services. I greeted every single person without taking a break. I wanted them to know that I appreciated everyone and their support. I was asked many times if I needed a break. I kept saying, "No." I was numb, but just kept going . . . I know that this was the man Rayco was and he would appreciate me being diligent . . . We received many letters, cards, flowers, food, calls, texts, visits, prayers from so many people. Rayco's wake and funeral were testaments to the devotion and dedication he had for his family, coworkers, his friends, my friends and even the young athletes he coached. I want to thank Rayco's fellow employees from Lightpath who came out in large numbers to Rayco's services. One of his co-workers who sat near him at work and would hear Rayco and me on the phone said, "Rayco and you were a true love story!" The coworkers still check on me periodically. I also want to thank my colleagues, who also came out in large numbers. They came out to support me. HS WEST is the best! My students were amazing. Those who couldn't drive, had their parents to accompany them. Many did not even know Rayco, or met him briefly on one or two occasions. I love each and every one of them who supported Rayco, me, and our family . . .

. . .

I know that if Rayco could see or know of all of these people paying respects to him, he would be so very humbled!

ONE OF THE TABLES OF CARDS...

This would be Rayco's expression after seeing all of the love people showed him . . .

THIS PIC WAS HUMBLING FOR ME . . . SO MANY PEOPLE CAME TO PAY THEIR RESPECTS!

24

Easter 2019

*R*ayco passed away exactly 10 years and 7 months after I lost my mom to cancer. I want to note that I was born on the 10th month and 7th day of a particular year...

On Easter weekend, our baby girl and her husband visited. They handed me a gift bag and said I must open it. I said, "Easter is for children." She said, "This year, it's for you as well, mom!" I opened the bag and read the card. I was startled, shocked, and overjoyed, all at the same time, to find out that they are pregnant!

Sometime later, LaniBani was sad, saying that her father will not know the baby. I explained that as believers in Christ, we know our spirit returns to him at passing from earth. His spirit and the baby's spirit are connecting. Later that night, she has a dream of her father's hands embracing her pregnant stomach. She was happy. After speaking with her, I said, "Thank you, God, for letting your Angel, my Rayco, embrace his new grandchild and show our baby girl that he is still around his family." God is good...

VICTORIA RAE WITH INDEX FINGER

My 3rd g-baby girl has her index finger up at 1 week old. She is letting the world know that she is the number one grandchild to see my Rayco in spirit . . . Her spirit met his in Heaven!

Easter Sunday, April 21, 2019

I went for extra prayer at the altar. I dared to go to a young couple. When I told my story, the woman cried. She said, "You came here for a reason." She told me to keep strong with my faith and I will be happy again. On Monday, April 22nd, a man called my phone asking for an item we put on Craig's List. I told him it was no longer available, but my husband had passed and we are selling other items. Was there anything else that he was looking for. He went on to say, "You will see him again." I said, "From your lips to God's ears." He said, "It is a fact." He asked if I had a Bible, I said, "Yes." He began to read Revelations 22:3-4 to me. He then said, "Yes, you are in pain now, but you will see him again." He later sent me more scriptures to read.

On Tuesday, April 22nd, I pick up the ringing phone. A telemarketer from LI Cares began to try and sell me. When I explained to her that I am not interested in anything she has to offer, I said that my husband had recently passed. She said, "I am so sorry for your loss." She then said, "You will see him again, not right away. It will be a long time from now. Just live your life. Have a good night." I hung up.

God used three different people, on three different days to tell me that I will see my Rayco again. In the Bible, it reads, on the 3rd day, Jesus arose from the dead. These messages from angels of God gave me hope. I love my Rayco so very much. His response to that was always ,"I love you more." I long to see him and hear him say again, "Love you more!"

25

Epilogue

Rayco's cousin traveled with me to see Jamaica several months after his passing. Rayco had originally made the reservations for the two of us to go in October for our 2019 birthdays to see where his family had lived. He made these reservations in January 2019. It was bittersweet traveling with his cousin, after Rayco's passing. However, I was grateful for her accompanying me . . . Jamaica's name for towns is Parish. Rayco's family lived in the Parish of Kingston. While there, she and I talked and prayed a lot. I must say it is God who has gotten me through this, along with the love of my children, grandchildren, Rayco's family, all of my friends and colleagues.

JAMAICA

Rayco's cousin wrote a beautiful letter to me while we were there. Part of the lines read:

"A part of who you are is gone, your identity is shaken to the core, you wonder if you will ever feel normal again. When you lose a mate, you lose part of yourself, it's as if you've had an amputation of a leg or an arm. You don't really recover you adjust and that process of adjusting varies with every individual. The pain that comes from the loss of a spouse is much deeper than most people realize because in a marital relationship, two people become one flesh. So when part of your flesh is abruptly taken away, there's a ripping and tearing that leaves a huge open wound. You had so many dreams and plans together, your future was anticipated as a twosome, you didn't do everything you had always hoped, the golden years won't be what you had imagined, some of the dreams have been dashed, you may feel completely hopeless and all you can see in your mind is ruined dreams . . . The only way you can have peace is to submit to the Lord and you do that by saying, 'OK, Lord, you brought me to this point in my life, what would you have me do next?'"

Rayco always would say, "Love you more," when we would text back and forth. He would also say that things happen for a reason. On our about April 3, 2019, I had to get the radiator in our bedroom repaired. After it was repaired, I had to put back some books that were stacked on a metal shelf in front of the radiator. I had stacked the books perfectly and one book fell again. I turned it around to read the front cover. It was untouched. This brand new journal was entitled "Love you more." I was speechless. This reminded me that I was loved deeply. I also loved my Rayco deeply. Our love will be a part of us forever—even though he is gone and I have to move toward a new life alone. I wrote this book as a testament of our love—that will remain forever—a timeless gift!

Several months before this book was published, I had a vision of Ray . . . Many people may not believe in visions. However, God and the visions he has sent me has kept me going…

Rayco and I were baptized in August 2018. The following August, I was attending one of my weekly Sunday church services. You see, staying close to GOD is the only thing that is keeping me STRONG! After church, a pleasant woman came over to greet our oldest daughter and myself. She asked, "Where is your hubby? I want to say hello to him…" I broke down. She always saw us in church together. She was confused. Carlzbear explained to her quietly that Rayco had passed . . . Several minutes later, an ordained minister, who happened to be visiting the church came over to me. She also happened to be my co-worker's mom. She sat with me and said to me, "Don't cry." She went on to say, "God wants you to know that he brought your husband to you so that you could travel through life together. God blessed you both with the capacity to love…It is better to have loved and lost than never to have loved at all!" I will always and forever love my Rayco. I know that he has always and forever loved me . . . MORE! THANK YOU GOD FOR BLESSING OUR UNION ON PLANET EARTH FOR OVER FOUR DECADES!!!!!

GRAFFITI RAYCO WROTE DURING OUR FINAL VACATION TOGETHER

During the month of October 2019, after I had visited where Rayco's family had lived in Jamaica and celebrated his life with his cousin, I had a vision. In the vision, Rayco was in bed with me. I remember saying to him, "Ray, you aren't here anymore. You have passed away. How are you in bed with me?" In the vision he said, "I will always be with you Nitagal!" This is a name he always called me. I felt comforted after the vision. I remember telling our first daughter and granddaughter about this when they came to say "good morning" to me the next day. I also remember that it was Sunday morning, because they had asked me what time would we be going to church. The vision gave me the strength to finish my book. It was very difficult to travel through memory lane. The vision was God's way of letting me know that Rayco's body may not be here, but he will "4 Ever" be with me in spirit!

Epilogue | 245

THE END . . . UNTIL WE MEET AGAIN!

Final Thoughts

This book was launched February 2020, approximately one month before the first year of Rayco's passing.

After reading this book, you will definitely recognize that I am a *numbers* person. My mom passed away in August 2008. I was born on the 10th month and 7th day of a certain year. My Rayco passed away exactly 10 years and 7 months after my mom..I was born on that calendar month and day, however, a part of my heart and soul also passed on that day Rayco passed, 10 years and 7 months after my mom . . . .

I want to also mention that on the 2019 into 2020 New Year, I had retired to bed approximately 12:40am. Rayco came to me again. His words were "Happy New Year, Nitagal . . . Remember I will always be with you" . . .

The first year of losing Rayco was beyond a nightmare. However, he has told me numerous times that he will always be with me. I BELIEVE THAT!

I have to mention and thank our adult children who during this first holiday without Rayco went above and beyond to show up and shout out for mom and each other!

My prayer is that this book, along with other things that I have put in place, ensures that our grandchildren . . . great-grandchildren . . . etc., always know who they are. You can only know who you are if you know your past, this is their past!

Thank you so very much again, for taking the time to read our legacy . . . God bless you and your family!